The CHAKRA
Workbook

The CHAKRA
Workbook

A Step-by-Step Guide to Realigning Your Body's Vital Energies

ANNA VOIGT

THUNDER BAY
P·R·E·S·S
SAN DIEGO, CALIFORNIA

Thunder Bay Press
An imprint of the Advantage Publishers Group
5880 Oberlin Drive, San Diego, CA 92121-4794
www.thunderbaybooks.com

All notations of errors or omissions should be addressed to Thunder Bay Press, Editorial Department, at the above address. All other correspondence (author inquiries, permissions) concerning the content of this book should be addressed to Lansdowne Publishing, Level 1, 18 Argyle Street, The Rocks NSW 2000, Australia.

ISBN 1-59223-039-3

Set in Stone Sans and Goudy on QuarkXPress
Printed in China
1 2 3 4 5   08 07 06 05 04

The Light that is in me greets the Light that is in you.
Om shree sache maha prabhu ki jai
Paramatma ki jai
Om shanti shanti shanti
Om
May the ultimate Truth be victorious.
May that which is beyond all boundaries be victorious.
May there be peace, peace, peace.

CONTENTS

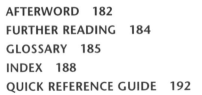

INTRODUCTION

Our senses and conscious minds perceive all beings as separate physical entities. Yet we are all interdependent beings in an interdependent multidimensional universe. Each person is an individualized microcosmic energy system. This system mirrors, interrelates with, and is interpenetrated by the macrocosmic energy system. To understand the way in which we are related to this universe, we need to see all of life as vibrations of energy.

Currents or waves of vibrational energy give rise to all material forms; the lower the frequency, the denser the form. A complex universal energy system is continuously at work, and it is this system that creates and sustains life. The force field of energy that fuels all energetic forms is both vast and constant. All currents of energy arise from and contain this force field and return to it, just as waves rise from the ocean and fall back into the ocean. As a law of physics states, energy is never lost; it is just transmuted from one state of being to another.

UNDERSTANDING THE ENERGETIC SYSTEM

Each of us has not only a physical body but also a subtle body. The subtle body is made of vital energy, the life force that animates the physical body. It is the seat of the mind. The subtle body is where we experience all of our ideas, emotions, feelings, and dreams. The systems of the subtle body provide paths for the vital universal energy (see Chapter Two).

Every thought, every emotion is a current of energy. Once we realize that all of our thoughts and all of our emotions are impacting on the energetic state of our being, we begin to see the importance of learning to understand how our minds and emotions are actually operating. We can then work to change that operation if it is not in our own and others' best interests—for in truth they are indivisible.

USING THIS WORKBOOK

In this workbook you will begin this journey of understanding by discovering how the energetic system works. You will learn about the chakras—the energetic centers of our bodies—and, in the process, how we affect others with our energy and are affected by theirs. You will also discover that amazing as the functioning of our physical systems are, the universe of which we are a part is even more awe inspiring.

This workbook will guide you through specific practices for each chakra in order to release energy blockages and rebalance disordered energy functioning. When regularly adhered to, these practices, along with healthy diets and moderate living, can cleanse and purify our entire system in preparation for and in support of the potential awakening of powerful spiritual energy. The practices can also bestow:

- an enhanced sense of well-being
- improved general health
- inner equanimity and balance
- greater self-knowledge
- expansion of consciousness

It is important to clarify your motivations, intentions, and goals at the beginning of taking up a healing or spiritual path. Write these down in a Daily Practice Workbook Journal along with your responses to the exercises and meditations throughout this book. Regularly revisit and revise your stated aspirations.

THE CHAKRAS

The word **chakra*** (or *cakra*) derives from Sanskrit and means "a wheel or a disk of energy." The term also encompasses the notion of a turning or spinning motion, as well as the process of transforming psycho-physical energy into spiritual energy. When spiritual energy is awakened in the body, it effects transformations in consciousness and changes in physiology. The chakras are integral to this subtle energetic process. They are transformational energy centers—energy transformers—in the subtle energy system of a human being. They are an integral part of the interface between the universal energy, or pure Consciousness, and the individual consciousness.

Chakras are not entities in themselves, but rather are pools or vortices of pranic energy. *Prana* is the vital life-force energy without which the physical body could not function. The pranic system, of which the chakras are an integral part, will be explained in greater detail in later chapters.

HARMONY OF THE ENERGIES

Like thoughts and emotions, the chakras cannot be seen as physical entities. However, through their association with particular elements, organs, and functions, they have a powerful effect upon the physical body. As well as having a key role in physical functioning, the chakras play a vital role in the embodiment of spiritual energy on the physical plane of existence. As such they are essential in the regulation of various states of consciousness, and are vital to the harmony of the energies within our entire beings.

ABOUT THE WORKBOOK EXERCISES

In your Daily Practice Workbook Journal record and periodically review:
- your responses to the practices described in this book
- your thoughts and feelings in response to the questions in this book

Allow yourself to be creative, in whatever form arises, in your responses.

*Terms described in the glossary (pages 185–187) are highlighted in **bold italic** the first time they are used.

AN ANCIENT AND LIVING TRADITION

Knowledge of the role of chakras in the transformation of energy and spiritual development came through the Eastern spiritual science of **yoga.** Yoga emerged from the Hindu religion, which is based on the ancient Indian scriptures called the Vedas.

Yoga is both an ancient and a living Hindu spiritual science and philosophy and one of the very few spiritual traditions that has maintained an unbroken development through thousands of years of history. The literal meaning of the Sanskrit word *yoga* is "union." It is derived from the old Sanskrit root, *yuga* or *yuj*, meaning "to yoke" or "harness." Yoga can mean "union" or "discipline," or both—yoking together body, mind, and soul in order to liberate the true Self.

Yoga has evolved into a system of practices to relax the body and mind, purify the system, and remove energy blockages. These practices prepare the practitioner for the ultimate purpose of yoga—to attain Self-realization or the spontaneous awakening, through Divine Grace, to his or her original nature—that of pure Consciousness. The chakras play a key role in this process.

Yoga was introduced into the West a little over a hundred years ago through visits from eminent Indian holy men such as Swami Vivekananda and Paramahansa Yogananda. Scholarly knowledge of yoga and the chakras also emerged through translations of the Vedas and other ancient Indian sacred texts. A few of these important translations are the now classic text on Kundalini, *The Serpent Power*, which includes a translation by Arthur Avalon (Sir John Woodroffe) of a classic Indian text, *The Shat-chakara-nirupana*; *The Siva Samhita* translated by K. Narayanaswami Aiyar; translations of the Upanishads; and the *Brahma-Sutras*. Helpful explanatory texts include *The Chakras*, written by theosophist and clairvoyant Charles W. Leadbeater. Leadbeater's text on the chakras and the subtle energetic system, based on his own experiences and an understanding of the traditional texts, became the most adopted in popular literature on the subject in the West

THE VEDAS

The **Vedas** are the world's most ancient spiritual texts. It is believed that the truths contained in all religions are derived from these texts. They are traditionally regarded as divine revelations from God to the great seer-poets (*kavi*) or Self-realized holy men of ancient India. The Vedic revelations were imparted to these sages through visionary episodes, ecstasies, and mystical insights.

Veda means knowledge or wisdom, and when used in conjunction with scriptures it means spiritual knowledge of eternal reality. The spiritual knowledge in the Vedas was initially handed down from generation to generation through oral transmission, and was subsequently written down around 5,000 years ago. The Vedas comprise four books— The Rig (or Rg) Veda, Sama Veda, Yajur Veda, and Atharva Veda. The oldest of the Vedas, and considered the most important, is the Rig Veda.

The essence of the Vedas was later compiled into volumes called the **Upanishads.** These, a continuation of the Vedic philosophy, discuss how the soul, the Atman, can be united with the One Ultimate Truth, **Brahman,** through meditation and by adhering to the law of **karma**—the universal law of cause and effect.

It is from the Upanishads that the practices of yoga derive. In around A.D. 150 the Indian sage Patanjali compiled a concise and comprehensive outline of the philosophy and practices of yoga called *The Yoga Sutras of Patanjali*. The *Yoga Sutras* has become a classic text for yoga practitioners. Another important Sanskrit text that is important to yoga practitioners is the *Bhagavad Gita* (the Song of God).

The arduous work done by translators and interpreters of complex ancient works—and the explanatory texts that have made such works accessible—continues to be invaluable to our understanding of the vast treasury of wisdom in Indian spirituality.

YOGA IN OUR TIMES

In our own times, knowledge of yoga has grown rapidly in the West, particularly through the teachings of Yoga Master Swami Sivananda Sarasvati and Yogacharya B. K. S. Iyengar, the preeminent proponents of a form of Tantra Yoga called Hatha Yoga (see page 16). It is from Tantra Yoga that the most comprehensive understanding is found of the human subtle anatomy, the chakra system, and Kundalini Shakti (see page 19), which is the energizing spiritual consciousness working through the chakra system.

BOTH REAL AND ILLUSORY

There has been much debate on whether the chakras are real, illusory, or just symbols of meditative focus on the spiritual path. Each has to answer this question according to individual experience. Also, the manifestations of Spirit in consciousness vary from person to person. Personal testimony already exists about actual experiences of the chakras. We could say they are at once real, illusory, and symbolic. They are real in the sense of being aspects of the subtle human anatomy and centers of vital energy—manifesting aspects of consciousness and patterns according to each individual's energetic functioning. These energetic patterns, or aspects of consciousness, are "knots" in consciousness that have to be untied for spiritual liberation to occur.

The chakras are illusory in that our underlying true Self may be seen as a free, unbound state of being, and anything on the surface of existence is ultimately illusory. They also act as powerful symbols of energy and points of focus in our work to release systemic energy blocks and so access liberating energy as we return to that ultimate free state of being of Self-realization.

CHAPTER ONE

YOGA AND CONSCIOUSNESS

Discover how you can explore consciousness through yoga. Learn about Shiva and Shakti. What are the different types of yoga? What is Kundalini? Where do you begin your journey of transformation through the chakras?

AN EXPLORATION OF CONSCIOUSNESS

In the West, leaps of understanding have usually come through the observation of physical and external forces and the manifestation of phenomena. In the East, great insights into the nature of existence have come through thousands of years of investigation into the inner planes of experiential reality and the links between mind and body in order to understand the nature of consciousness.

Essentially, all true forms of yoga, such as Tantra Yoga, are explorations of consciousness—of understanding its manifestations and applying techniques to expand the conscious experience. For thousands of years Tantra Yoga has been studying the consciousness of individual human beings and the way the consciousness responds when a person willingly subjects the body–mind to techniques to discipline and direct it and expand consciousness beyond its known limits. The yoga techniques were handed down by yoga masters—*rishis, swamis, yogis, yoginis,* sages—who had already experienced the path to Self-realization and were therefore able to guide others through the perils, as well as recognizing a seeker's genuine unfolding. The goal of these explorations has been the experience and attainment of the Oneness of pure Consciousness beyond the boundaries of time and space. Aeons before scientists discovered that material form is actually energy vibrating at a certain rate, the yogis and rishis of India already understood that the human body–mind was a manifestation of the greater creative power of the Universe.

SHAKTI

Unlike the scientists, who perceive energy simply as energy vibrating into matter, the yogis consider energy as consciousness and matter as its vehicle. This dynamic power is seen to be inherently sacred and is known as *Shakti,* the Divine Feminine, the Divine Mother, who is the creative aspect of the ultimate reality, the formless principle that underpins and permeates all existence.

THE DANCE OF SHIVA AND SHAKTI

It is said that Tantra Yoga was created and taught to humankind by the Lord **Shiva.** Shiva is one of the three principal Gods of Indian spirituality. He forms part of the *Trimurti,* the Hindu Trinity, of Brahma, the Creator; *Vishnu,* the Preserver; and Shiva, the Destroyer. These deities reflect the three aspects of phenomenal reality. The Tantra Yoga that Shiva taught to humankind shows how a person can transform and transcend the individual consciousness and reach a state of Oneness with the Supreme Consciousness.

The individual's dance of energy with the cosmos is exquisitely personified in the Hindu pantheon as the Dance of Shiva and Shakti. Shiva is the great formless Energy, portrayed as male, and Shakti is the creative power, portrayed as female. The dance represents the attainment of eternal bliss: the divine union of the individually created soul with impersonal, formless Energy, whence Shakti sprang. It represents Self-realization, the goal of all spiritual practices.

TANTRA YOGA is a combination of the four principal yogas: Hatha Yoga, Mantra Yoga, Laya Yoga, and Raja Yoga. Each offers a systematic pathway for reaching a state of *samadhi* (blissful union with the Self). Each pathway places meditation at the center of its essential practices for spiritual attainment. Practices and exercises from all of these modalities are included throughout this book.

HATHA YOGA is the most widely known and practiced form of Tantra Yoga in the West. *Hatha* expresses the perennial polarities of existence. *Ha* is the active or positive principle of existence, symbolized by the sun, heat, light, and creativity. *Tha* is the reflective, or negative, principle, symbolized by the moon, cold, darkness, and receptivity. Hatha also refers to the *nadis* of the subtle body through which prana flows. Nadis (see Chapter Two) form the system of energy channels or conduits for prana. Knowledge of the human subtle energy system is fundamental to the *asanas* (postures) and *pranayama* (conscious breath control), the purificatory practices of Hatha Yoga.

MANTRA YOGA uses practices in *mantra japa* (mantra recitation) to control the mind and develop concentration. The Universe is created from *nada-bindu* (primordial sound), hence sound practices are a vital aspect of invoking Divine Consciousness. Through regular *mantra* repetition a seeker can enter deeper into meditation and attain steady concentration, as well as invoking the divine form of Kundalini Shakti.

LAYA YOGA is also called Kundalini Yoga. At its core are methods for arousing the dormant Kundalini Shakti in the first chakra and uniting her with Paramashiva (Shiva in his highest aspect) in the seventh chakra. (Chapters Four to Ten describe the process.)

RAJA YOGA, however, does not awaken Kundalini. Instead, it focuses attention on arresting the thinking apparatus through concentrated attention and purifying the consciousness to attain the withdrawal of sensory perceptions (as in the state of deep sleep), leading to deep meditation and absorption in the Supreme Consciousness.

UNDERSTANDING TANTRA YOGA

There has been considerable misinterpretation, misunderstanding, and misapplication of Tantra Yoga in the West. More often than not it has become identified with hedonistic or healing sexual practices. However, the sexual practice rites of Tantra Yoga are only one of its aspects and are called the "Left-hand Path of Tantra." "Left hand" does not imply anything at all sinister—this was erroneously believed in the West because of propaganda and superstition in the Middle Ages. "Left" in Tantra Yoga means female, magnetic, emotional, and visual in nature. Recognizing the powerful expression of energy that is sexuality, the sexual rites of this path are utilized to arouse energy to stimulate spiritual energy in order to calm the active and restless mind and make it one-pointed in focus of attention. When sexual intercourse is used, it is a means to arouse the dormant Kundalini Shakti. Techniques are also employed to stop ejaculation and direct seminal fluid, along with vaginal fluid, upward to the Soma chakra.

This form of yoga is sometimes difficult for Western people to accept, even in theory, because of cultural conditioning about sexuality. Nonetheless, the goal and practices of this form of yoga (not covered in this book) are always directed toward the attainment of spiritual consciousness.

A PATH OF TRANSFORMATION

The human body–mind as an energetic microcosm of the cosmic macrocosm was understood by yogis to be the perfect vehicle for understanding the workings of the cosmos: for understanding the "mind of God" within all of creation. The goal was to:

- come to know our own consciousness experientially
- know how we all create our perceptions of reality through conditioned patterns of thought, emotion, and behavior
- know how we can, through systematic practices, untie ourselves from this conditioning to connect to and come to know the true Self, the greater reality in Oneself

The yogis realized that to discover the true Self, we have to direct and control the attention because the energy of the body–mind follows attention. The focuses we choose for our attention create patterns of energy, and these cause habits of thought and behavior that can become obstructive and harmful to the search for real happiness and freedom. Yoga techniques and inquiry focus the attention on the true Self, or the Divine, until the apparatus of attention is freed from the habits of the body–mind and established in the Self. It is then that we become truly alive, responding to the moment in the free unbounded space of Self-realized being.

This is the path of yoga, Tantra Yoga, and chakra work. It is a path of the transformation and transmutation of a contaminated habituated individual consciousness, bound by time and space, to the pure Consciousness of the Self beyond time and space.

KUNDALINI AND THE CHAKRAS

At the core of the path of Tantra, or Kundalini, Yoga is the awakening of the dormant spiritual energy in human beings and its rise through the chakras, culminating in the attainment of Self-realization. This dormant spiritual energy in Tantra Yoga is known as **Kundalini,** or **Kundalini Shakti.** As mentioned earlier, the dynamic creative principle of the Universe is known in Hinduism and yoga as Shakti. Shakti has many names and forms, as will be seen in the discussions of the chakras throughout this book.

Kundalini is in itself a vast subject covering many different levels. However, in brief, Kundalini Shakti is the spiritualizing energy or power that lies dormant in human beings and can be awakened through specific and systematic spiritually directed practices. Traditionally, the knowledge of Kundalini Shakti has been a closely guarded secret revealed only by a Master to a few select initiates.

Although the term "Kundalini" or "Kundalini Shakti" comes from the Tantra Yoga traditions, a phenomenon akin to the Kundalini experience is recognized in all of the shamanic traditions and mystical paths, in nearly all of the world's major religions, and in genuine occult traditions. All of these traditions recognize the significance of Kundalini as a key to "divinizing" or "spiritualizing" a human being. From the perspective of an individual spiritual seeker, it is a path to enlightenment, liberation, or Self-realization. In Sanskrit, *kundalini* is the feminine form of *kandala*, meaning "coiled" or "ring." The meaning of *kundalini* is "she who is coiled." The Tantra traditions conceive of Kundalini as Shakti (Power) in the image of a serpent and as the dynamic feminine aspect of Shiva, who is pure Consciousness.

JOURNEY THROUGH THE CHAKRAS

When the Kundalini awakens—usually after a long period of preparatory practices—she rises from her dormant state at the base of the **Muladhara** (first) chakra and rises through the chakras, piercing them as she goes and rendering them inert. The chakras are integral to the transforming of psycho-physical energy into spiritual energy. This is the path of Kundalini Shakti and of spiritual reawakening in Self-realization.

There are numerous testimonials of Kundalini experiences. However, we must always come back to our own experience on the spiritual path, for herein lies the only true knowledge. Knowing a concept does not mean that we "know." Intellectual knowledge is partial and surface knowledge and can even get in the way of an ability to recognize Truth and know it experientially. It is also important to bear in mind that individual experiences vary and the spiritual realm is not a textbook. So it is crucial that we learn to recognize Truth in ourselves honestly. Also, bear in mind that certain ideas may not make sense until you have had enough experience to integrate further understanding. Let the Light be your guide, or as the Buddha said to his close followers, "Be a Light unto your Self."

WORKBOOK EXERCISES

Following is a list of questions to expand awareness, guide you toward greater self-knowledge, and help you develop insight into living with more enduring happiness. In your Workbook Journal, write down, without any censorship, the thoughts and feelings that arise in response to these questions. Try not to force responses but ask yourself each question and note what arises.

1. How do we know what we know?
2. How do we know that our current conceptual understanding of ourselves, humankind, and creation is true?
3. The ways in which we live today and the knowledge now available to us are different from that of our ancestors. How do you imagine future generations will view our times?
4. What do you think fundamentally propels such change?
5. If our current conceptual models are sound and we know we all want peace of mind and healthy, happy, fulfilled lives, why is there so much physical, emotional, and psychic suffering in our world today?
6. List five people you consider to be good role models for humanity. What qualities guided your choices?
7. Ask yourself "Who am I?" and note what arises in response to this question.
8. What do you perceive is the purpose of your life on Earth?
9. List ten ethical principles and values that guide your everyday life.
10. List five factors that provide you with a sense of foundational support in your life.
11. List eight areas that give you a sense of connection to life.
12. List five factors that give you a sense of community.
13. If you feel alienated from community, list the reasons why.
14. List ten qualities that most describe your energetic state of being at this time.

CHAPTER TWO

THE HUMAN ENERGY SYSTEM

Discover the subtle bodies in the human energy system. What are the koshas?
How does prana work? What are auras? What are the nadis and where are the
major nadis located?

To be able to work effectively toward clearing our chakra systems and to awaken to higher dimensions of consciousness, we need to accept the reality of these vital concepts:

- the multidimensional nature of a human being
- the human energy system
- the functioning of subtle energies within a human being

This book explores the subtle energy system, or subtle anatomy, as the chakras are located within it. And it is through this system that the dormant Kundalini Shakti wakes and rises up through the chakras, piercing and transforming their energies to unite with Shiva in Self-realization. The subtle energy system consists basically of the following dimensions or aspects:

- the subtle bodies—the **koshas,** or sheaths
- the aura
- the nadis, or channels of prana (vital energy or life force)
- the chakras, or subtle centers of vital energy

THE FIVE KOSHAS

According to the ancient teachings of the Upanishads, the human body is just the outermost level, or layer, of the multidimensional organism that constitutes a human being. Teachings in the Taittiriya Upanishad reveal that a human exists simultaneously on five levels, the *koshas*—the five sheaths of consciousness:

1. The "envelope consisting of food," or "sheath of matter," known in Sanskrit as *Anna-maya (or anna-mayi) kosha*—the **cellular body.** (Spelling differs in various texts: *maya* and *mayi* are used interchangeably for all koshas.) With the assistance of prana, the vital life-force energy, this sheath creates the foundation of the physical body. All material contents of the physical body–mind are created by prana, but the material contents evolve through food.

2. The "envelope consisting of life-force," or "sheath of vital air" (prana), known as *Prana-maya-kosha*. This is the **bioenergetic field** surrounding the physical body. It sustains the individual consciousness and all mental, superconscious, and psychic energy. The life-force in the cellular body is maintained by prana through food, which is converted into different kinds of energy. This sheath, called the **etheric body** by Charles W. Leadbeater, contains the chakra system. All the other sheaths interpenetrate with this sheath and accordingly are affected by the chakras it contains.

3. The "envelope consisting of mind," or "sheath of mind," is called *Mano-maya-kosha*. This refers to the "lower" mind, which processes all sensory information. It is also known as the **astral body,** or **emotional body.** Prana also maintains the vitality in this sheath through the chemical ingredients prepared by the "sheath of matter," which create different moods, emotions, and feelings in the individual consciousness. This variety of moods, emotions, and feelings in interaction with the individual consciousness gives a definite character to each human organism.

4. The "envelope consisting of intelligence," or "sheath of knowledge," is called *Vijnana-maya-kosha*. It is also known as the **mental body.** This sheath is the seat of the "higher mind" or intellect, and the "I-consciousness," or ego (**ahamkara**)—that knowledge beyond sensory input that generates understanding and wisdom. In individual consciousness, the intellect and the ego are bound by time and perceive through the time sequences of past, present, and future. In this interplay between the intellect and the ego, the mind gives messages from the sensory world to the intellect, which holds a record of all that has happened in the past and accordingly projects future possibilities. The intellect is conscious of the so-called "positive" and "negative" aspects of all that is presented by the mind.

5. The "envelope consisting of bliss," or "sheath of bliss," is known as *Ananda-maya-kosha*. It is also known as the **causal,** or **spiritual, body.** This is the energetic field through which the individual connects with ultimate reality—the eternal Self. The Self is the pure Consciousness in individual consciousness. It is inherently blissful and is beyond ego, time, and intellect. The Self is unmoved by the pleasure and pain of transient existence and remains in *ananda* (bliss) in its own sheath at the same time as transcending the five sheaths or envelopes. The Self is the nondual Cosmic Consciousness—the One Consciousness of all that is. In nonduality there is no separation of Self and "other"—all is One. While remaining in its own sheath, the *Ananda-maya-kosha* is omnipresent, omnipotent, and omniscient.

Each of the body–minds, or sheaths, possesses its own fundamental vibrational frequency. The etheric body, which is closest to the physical body, vibrates with the lowest frequency. The astral/emotional and mental bodies have higher frequencies, and the causal/spiritual body has the highest frequency of all. (Body–mind refers to each "body" within us, both material and subtle, and its processes and particular aspects of consciousness.)

THE CHAKRAS IN THE SUBTLE BODY SYSTEM

Some yoga and chakra texts differ on the location of the chakras in the subtle body system. Some place the chakras in *prana-maya-kosha*, the sheath of vital air, or etheric body, and others locate them in *mano-maya-kosha*, the sheath of mind, or astral body. However, the different placements of the chakras does not affect the practices or the outcomes involved in chakra work. The chakras are an integral part of the subtle energy anatomy, which is aligned with the physical anatomy, and references to their approximate positions in relation to certain areas and organs in the physical body are similar in most texts.

Each of the five sheaths, or body–minds, exists and operates in different dimensions, but rather than existing separately, they are interacting parts of an organic whole. Prana is the essential energy that enables connection between the subtle and the material/physical levels of the human organism. It activates all of the systems in the body and helps them work together as necessary. Each body–mind is maintained by the type of prana needed for and appropriate to that dimension.

The subtle energetic sheath enveloping the physical body is the location of the nadis—the pranic conduits, or pathways, in which prana circulates and where the chakras (the energy-transforming centers) are situated. It is within this subtle pranic system that the Kundalini Shakti, the potentially transforming Divine Mother Energy, lies dormant (see Chapter One, "Kundalini and the Chakras," and see also Chapters Four to Ten).

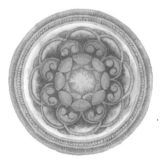

THE FIVE SHEATHS AND PRANA

The vast force field of energy that sustains life is known as *prana*, Sanskrit for "vital life-force" or "vital energy." Prana maintains life, material form, and consciousness. It is the carrier of the vital life-sustaining energy and the energy necessary for excreting toxins and chemical wastes from the body. The level of consciousness of every living being depends on the frequencies of prana it is capable of absorbing and storing. Generally speaking, animals have lower frequencies than humans, and humans advanced in awareness have higher frequencies than those beginning their spiritual journey.

Prana is also known in the languages of other cultures, for example *ch'i, qi,* or *ki* in Chinese—as in tai chi, or qi gong. All systems that consciously work with prana, or ki, are concerned with cultivating a healthy flow of this vital energy. The ultimate aim of all of these paths is transcendent union with the Self—the One known by many names. Knowledge of prana has been documented in the Vedas and the Upanishads and is fundamental to an understanding of yoga and chakra practices.

Based on the wisdom of the Upanishads and the experiences of adepts, Tantra Yoga teaches that prana is the gateway to the spiritual realm. And each body–mind—except for the "sheath of bliss," or causal/spiritual body—is maintained by the type of prana necessary to its particular dimension. Consequently, Tantra Yoga places the utmost emphasis on working with the dynamic prana energy that the human organism receives through nasal breathing. Through conscious breath control techniques called pranayama, based on the understanding of various prana currents, prana is regulated and utilized to cleanse the nerves and arouse the dormant Kundalini Shakti.

Prana is sometimes referred to as the breath itself. However, it is a very subtle energy that can be perceived only by a very sensitive yoga adept. Most of us only perceive prana as the living form with which it has established a connection, such as the breath, sound, color, or material form.

WORKING WITH PRANA

In the course of spiritual development, it is necessary to evolve systematically through all dimensions, gradually increasing awareness of the higher reaches of consciousness. In this way we can transcend the limitations of the body–minds and ultimately enter into divine union with the true Self or the One abiding principle.

Only the pure being of individualized consciousness is able to experience the Consciousness of the "sheath of bliss," the *ananda-maya-kosha*. This sheath of blissfully energized Consciousness cannot be reached by the mind or even by prana. The first four body–mind systems—the physical, the etheric, the astral/emotional, and the mental—are energized by prana. The vicissitudes, confusions, limitations, and troubles of life are found within these body–minds.

Prana supports both cellular and mental energy. Cellular energy is subject to changes, and influences mental energy through the various moods, emotions, and feelings. Mental energy then influences the ego and the intellect. When the ego wearies of the incessant interchange of mental energy, it needs rest. For most human beings it only seems possible to rest from mental processes when we are in a deep sleep. However, sleep is often interrupted by dreams, which involve mental energy, and therefore does not always remain deep. For complete rest we need to stop the mind as well as the body.

As the mind is dependent on prana for its activity, the only answer is to control pranic energy and stop prana. Through the practices of yoga—meditation, concentration, mantra repetition, postures (*asanas*), breath control (*pranayama*), and gestures (**mudras**)—we can learn the techniques of working with prana. This is why these practices are of such fundamental importance in psycho-spiritual integration and the opening to Self-realization.

THE AURA

In the West, the fields of the subtle bodies have come to be called the *auras*, which are reservoirs of subtle energy for a specific range of frequencies. They are generated by the totality of our internal energetic processes. The ethereal or "etheric" body, the mental body, and the causal or spiritual body all have surrounding "egg-shaped" auras. The aura of the ethereal body is sometimes called the **health aura**, because the conditions of the physical body and the energy radiation of the ethereal body are closely related. This etheric field is said to hold a living database of our experiences through time, including, some say, former lives. Unresolved traumas, such as unhealed psychic wounds, unfinished communications, and other unfinished business, are believed to leave their trace in the aura. Some also believe that premonitions are revealed through this field.

Disease will manifest in the ethereal aura before becoming apparent in the physical body. The ethereal aura also shows disturbances in the physical body, and it is this aura that is "read" by psychics and medical intuitives as an indicator of disturbed or damaged areas in the physical body. It is this aura that is usually referred to in Western texts.

THE PERSONAL AURA

Each person has a personal aura, which is an amalgamation of the etheric, the emotional/astral, the mental, and causal/spiritual bodies. We often have instant responses to a person's energetic "feel"—and vaguely like or dislike that person accordingly. This is a response to the person's aura.

As auras or subtle energy fields operate according to frequencies, they attract and reject similar frequencies. This accounts for the like-attracts-like principle—even though this may not be apparent to our conscious minds. The frequencies will reflect our actual state of being, not our constructed self-image or persona, which may be based on rejecting aspects of ourselves we do not want to accept. Accordingly, those we attract, but whom we may not consciously like, may be reflecting disowned or unconscious aspects of ourselves. Our outer circumstances act as a mirror to our internal state, which is immensely useful, if sometimes challenging, on our journey toward wholeness.

MORE ABOUT AURAS

In addition to personal auras, there are collective auras—for example, when people come together in a group or crowd. Here personal auras combine to form a collective aura that we perceive as the "mood of the group." This can in part explain the magnetic pull of the "group mind," and why people can be drawn into behaving in groups in ways that they may ordinarily reject. This collective aura, as with all things, can operate toward beneficial or harmful outcomes.

Kirlian photography, which makes visible the activity of the auric field, has revealed some fascinating things about the etheric body. For example, Kirlian photographs show that even when parts of a tree leaf have been removed, the etheric body of the leaf remains almost the same. This could perhaps explain the "phantom limb" phenomenon of amputees who frequently talk about having sensation in a severed limb.

WORKBOOK EXERCISES

1. Reflect on a time you have met someone you instantly liked and on a time you have met someone you instantly disliked. Were those impressions later clarified and confirmed? Write down three qualities you immediately liked/disliked about this person. Now look honestly at each of these qualities in yourself. What do you perceive? Write down your reflections in your Workbook Journal.
2. In your daily life, start becoming more aware of your reactions and responses—sensations, thoughts, feelings, sensings—to different people and different situations, whether familiar or unfamiliar. Write down some of your responses in your Workbook Journal, particularly those that produce a stronger energetic charge.

THE NADIS

Both the physical and subtle bodies contain a certain number of **nadis.** The word nadi comes from the Sanskrit root *nad,* which means movement. In the most ancient Hindu scripture, the Rig Veda, *nadi* is used to mean "stream." The nadis are understood as a network of channels or conduits of energy in the subtle anatomy. The function of the nadis is to transport prana throughout a person's subtle energy system. Accordingly, the nadis are channels for pranic energy. Nadis can be likened to the meridians of Chinese medicine.

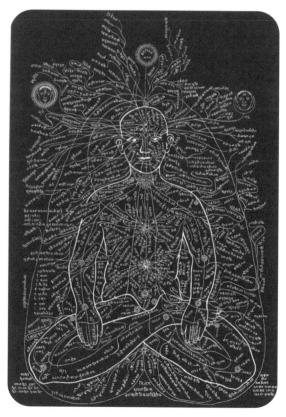

Some teachings cite as many as 340,000, though the number that appears most frequently is 72,000. Nonetheless, all available teachings speak of ten, twelve, or fourteen nadis as being more important than the rest. In all of the teachings, particular significance is accorded to the three major nadis—the **Sushumna Nadi** (and the **Brahma Nadi** inside the Sushumna Nadi), the **Ida Nadi,** and the **Pingala Nadi.**

The Upanishads concur that the nadis originate in the navel—in a spherical region called the **kanda** (or *kandasthana* in Sanskrit). The egg-shaped kanda centers around the navel and from there the nadis spread out over and beyond the entire body. This network of nadi currents has been likened by yoga adepts and clairvoyants to a tree of illumined filaments.

THE THREE MAJOR NADIS

The most important nadis for Kundalini Yoga practitioners are the three major nadis—the Sushumna, the Ida, and the Pingala. These nadis are identified with the three major rivers of India. All of the nadis merge at the **Sahasrara**—the crown, or seventh—chakra. The Ida Nadi and Pingala Nadi convey the inhalation and exhalation of nasal breathing associated with prana and *apana,* and also all the subtle energy of the body.

THE SUSHUMNA NADI

In the Upanishads and other sources, the Sushumna (or Susumna) Nadi is in the central canal of the spinal cord and has an opening, the gate of Brahman, at the Sahasrara chakra. The Sushumna Nadi runs the entire length of the spinal column and is the only nadi that passes through this column. The Kundalini Shakti rises through the Sushumna Nadi channel to meet her Lord Shiva. This meeting is symbolic of the blissful union of the individual consciousness with the Divine Cosmic Consciousness in Self-realization.

Most yoga and Tantric scriptures appear to concur that the Sushumna Nadi originates in the Muladhara (root/first) chakra, situated in the perineum at the base of the spine, and terminates at the Sahasrara chakra, at the crown of the head—through which prana and the Kundalini Shakti are believed to enter and exit. It is the seat of **OM (AUM)**, the source of all sound, the sacred syllable seed sound that continues infinitely (see Chapters Nine and Ten).

It is said that the Sushumna Nadi, rather than being one nadi, is made up of three principal nadis and is the most subtle of all the nadis. Inside the flame-red outer part of the Sushumna Nadi is the Vajrini, or Vajra, Nadi, associated with the sun. Inside the Vajrini is the Chitrini, or Chitra, Nadi, associated with the moon, said to be as "subtle as a spider's thread." The space within Chitrini is called the Brahma Nadi, "the channel of the Absolute." It is the conduit for the Kundalini Shakti to the gate of Brahman, through which she ascends to the Sahasrara chakra. Such is the intricate pathway of Kundalini Shakti's ascent to her final abode and her blissful return to Oneness in reunion with her beloved Shiva.

ACTIVATING THE SUSHUMNA NADI

The Sushumna Nadi is the only nadi that is beyond the limits of time. It usually remains dormant while prana is flowing through the other nadis, and is activated when pranic flow through the other nadis is curtailed—such as in pranayama (breath control) practices. It is activated only when the breath comes through both nostrils simultaneously—though this does not activate the Brahma Nadi, carrier of spiritual energy.

THE IDA NADI

The Ida Nadi is the prana channel on the left of the Sushumna Nadi. It is also called the "moon nadi," carrying the lunar energy currents. Ida Nadi is white or a pale silvery color and is cooling and calming—conserving energy in the body and restoring equanimity to the mind. Ida is considered feminine and receptive in nature and is also called Ganga— referring to the Ganges River, treasured in India as Mother.

Ida Nadi is the treasury of maternal energy and nurtures and purifies the body–mind. The Ida Nadi can be seen as the yin of the yogic energetic system. It terminates in the left nostril and is associated with the left breath—that is, when breath is flowing in and out of the left nostril. All pranayama practices commence with inhalation through the left nostril, which activates Ida Nadi. (*Tha* of Hatha Yoga is connected with Ida Nadi. See page 16.)

THE PINGALA NADI

The Pingala Nadi is the prana channel on the right side of the Sushumna Nadi. It is also known as the "sun nadi," carrying the solar currents, and is seen as masculine and active. The Pingala Nadi is hot, like the sun, and stores energy that is used in physical activities requiring muscular strength, speed, and physical power. Where Ida Nadi is seen as gentle, Pingala Nadi is seen as strong. The Pingala Nadi is associated with the sacred Indian river Yamuna. The Pingala Nadi can be seen as the yang of the yogic energetic system. It terminates in the right nostril and is associated with the right breath—that is, when breath is flowing in and out of the right nostril.

DAYTIME AND NIGHTTIME BREATHING

Pingala Nadi as solar is identified with daytime and Ida Nadi as lunar with nighttime. Interestingly, yogis work toward reversing this normal process and practice keeping Ida Nadi open in the daytime and Pingala Nadi open at night to increase vitality. (*Ha* of Hatha Yoga is connected to Pingala Nadi. See page 16.)

 ## WORKBOOK EXERCISES

1. Although the human subtle anatomy is specific in its functioning, it is sometimes helpful to play with concepts visually and creatively—as we can with aspects of the human physical anatomy—in ways that are more personally meaningful. Illustrate creatively in your Workbook Journal:
   • the five koshas, or sheaths
   • the kanda
   • the Sushumna Nadi
2. The Ida Nadi is known as the "moon nadi," carrying the lunar energy currents in the body. Write or draw three ways you can creatively imagine lunar energy in your body and in your consciousness.
3. The Pingala Nadi is known as the "sun nadi," carrying the solar energy currents in the body. Write or draw three ways you can creatively imagine solar energy in your body and in your consciousness.
4. Auras are associated with colors. Imagine a color for the aura of four people you know and for yourself. Why did you come up with those particular colors?
5. What have you learned about the subtle energy system within a human being? Make a list of how you can use this knowledge in your own life.

CHAPTER THREE

OUTLINE OF THE CHAKRAS

What are the chakras? Discover the tattwas, the lotus symbol, the bija mantra, and the yantra. Which yoga postures are suitable for meditation? Learn how to prepare yourself for chakra work.

The chakras are spinning wheels or vortices of vital energy. They are extremely subtle centers of energy in the Brahma Nadi, a very fine nadi and vehicle of spiritual energy within the Sushumna Nadi (see page 31).

Even though we may not be aware of them, the chakras are always active. They are said to have a location in the body (see Figure 8), even though they exist in the subtle body and not in the physical body. The locations can vary slightly from person to person, but the chakras remain consistent in their ascending order and in their relationship to each other.

SENSING THE CHAKRAS

Although the chakras are not physical entities observable with normal vision, there are accounts of their structure and colors from yogis who have "seen" them clairvoyantly. The chakras can also be sensed, and they are evident in the shape of our physical bodies, which indicate our behavioral patterns—the way we think, feel, behave, react to our life circumstances, and relate to others. Our awareness of the chakras can be likened to our awareness of the wind, in that we cannot "see" it, but know its presence by its movement against objects. We know the feel of it brushing against our skin and in the swirling movement of tree branches and the shivering movement of leaves.

THE UPPER AND LOWER CHAKRAS

The chakras have become associated with various states of consciousness, depending on their location in the physical body. They are also associated with archetypal patterns and psychological and philosophical concepts. For example, the lower chakras, closer to the Earth, are related to the physical and practical aspects of our lives. The upper chakras represent mental realms and higher states of awareness and expression and work on more symbolic levels through language, images, and concepts. The chakras can also be seen as a developmental map of human maturation, from infancy to old age, as well as a pictograph of psycho-spiritual integration.

In the West, more value is often attached to the concepts relating to the upper rather than the lower chakras. This most likely stems from the practice in some Western religions of seeing the Spirit and the body as separate. In some cases this means less value is attributed to the Earth and the physical body and causes a tendency to want to *transcend* the physical, rather than consciously *embodying* the spiritual dimension. In actuality, all of the chakras have important roles to play in psycho-spiritual integration. The queen operative of the yogic system of awakening, Kundalini Shakti, lies sleeping in the lowest chakra, the Muladhara. Retaining a complete equality of attitude toward the upper and lower chakras is important on this spiritual path.

LINKS WITH OTHER BELIEF SYSTEMS

The chakras could be likened to the proverbial Tree of Life, the staircase to Heaven, or a type of "Jacob's ladder" connecting the polarities of Heaven and Earth, Spirit and matter, mind and body, female and male. We could see these polarities as existing on a continuum, with each chakra as an axis of a tree branch or a step on the ladder—the incremental steps that are intrinsic to all of life's processes. Each ascending step would move the individual from a seemingly solid, well-defined, low-frequency vibrational state to a higher frequency, more subtle vibrational state, and an increasingly freer form of being. Each descending step, in contrast, would bring us to more solid forms. Yet the process is circular, too. The journey up and the journey down can both lead to spiritual awakening.

THE TATTWAS (TATTVAS)

As energy descends in vibration from the subtle higher frequencies into the lower frequencies of material form, it manifests as particular elements called **tattwas.** The tattwas are principles of Creation, and there are said to be thirty-six of them. Those related to the chakras are the tattwas of materiality—the elements of earth, water, fire, air, and **akasha** (space/ether). These elements represent the greatest degree of contraction of energy of all the tattwas. Although these five elements are found throughout the body, they have centers of concentration in their corresponding chakras. The influences of these five tattwas or elements are represented in the pictograph of each chakra by the particular shape of that element—which is known as the **yantra.** (See Figures 1–7 and Chapters Four to Ten for a description of the yantra of each chakra.)

The elements also represent the universal principles of Creation. Knowing the association between the elements and principles of Creation will help you understand the distinctive nature of each chakra.

Symbol	Element	Universal principle it represents
☐	Earth	Gravity
☽	Water	Polarity
▽	Fire	Combustion
✡	Air	Equilibrium
◯	Akasha/ether	Vibration

THE LOTUS

In traditional accounts, each chakra is described in the form of a *padma*—lotus—with a particular number of petals. The lotus petals are the seats of modes of our being and their connected desires, which are maintained by the functioning of the senses. Each of the first five chakras is influenced by a particular *tattwa*, or element, and is connected to a particular sense and its related sense organ—the nose, the tongue, the eyes, the skin, or the ears (see Vishnu, pages 86–87, for more about the lotus symbol).

THE LOTUS PETALS

On each lotus petal is inscribed a letter and a sound from the Sanskrit alphabet representing a sound that has emerged from primordial sound (**Nada Brahma** or **Sabda Brahman**). The Sanskrit letters are also the seats of "mental modifications," or states of mind and related desires, which are maintained by the functioning of the five senses.

The lotus petals are said to point downward, causing energy to flow down, but when the Kundalini Shakti rises, they go up like a lotus in bloom. Within the lotus are the presiding deities   aspects of Kundalini Shakti and Lord Shiva, who is one of the principal deities in Hinduism and an aspect of the *Trimurti*, or Hindu Trinity.

BIJA MANTRA (SEED SOUND)

Each petal of a lotus, or chakra, has a **bija mantra,** or seed sound, associated with it. The bija mantra, as the late Yoga Master Harish Johari describes it, is "a storehouse of divinity in a most concentrated form." The sound frequencies of the bija mantra are used to invoke the Divine energy inside the body. When the sound is produced in a correct manner, the latent power of the Divinity is aroused. The yoga system perceives that all that exists in the universe, from material form to mental activity, consists of sounds of varying concentration, frequency, and wavelength.

THE YANTRA

Within the lotus, which is represented as a circle, is a yantra—the particular symbolic shape of an element. It is the visual equivalent of the chanted seed sound. Yantra diagrams are metaphysical symbols, not just visual designs. Each aspect of a yantra has a universal plane of meaning. Sometimes called a "power diagram," the yantra is a means by which the physics and metaphysics of the world are invoked through meditation to synchronize with the psyche of the meditator. In other words, when a yantra is regularly meditated upon in a systematic manner, the meditator becomes attuned to the vibrations the yantra holds, and her or his consciousness is drawn to the planes the yantra symbolically represents.

THE CHAKRAS: RENEWING OUR ENERGIES

As we grow from infancy we begin to perceive ourselves and other beings as separate. We rely on external information and our rational minds for our sense of "reality" and self-identity; we lose awareness of the Oneness of nature. This is reinforced by social conditioning, where different life forms are usually treated as entirely separate entities.

With this perception of separateness comes fear, which manifests in a host of ways. In the West, fears of separation can reach an apex in a fear of death, which is seen as the annihilation of the self. Death of the physical self may be perceived as the end of life. Understanding the chakras will help us understand that our true nature is Oneness of Being with the Divine, the One Consciousness that dwells within us all and all Creation.

Most Eastern spiritual paths incorporate purification practices, but they do not specifically incorporate chakra cleansing practices. This is characteristic of the paths of Tantra Yoga, where purification practices cleanse the system and release blocked energy. This reestablishes the natural rhythm of vital energy flow and reconnects us to the cosmic energy flow of life. Energy that has been blocked becomes stagnant and, like a stagnant pond, attracts and breeds impurities and toxins. This weakens the entire system, which increases the risk of disease and systemic disorders—physical, emotional, psychological, and spiritual. When we commit to a regular chakra practice routine, we will in time begin to feel refreshed and renewed. True wholeness of being is the goal of chakra-clearing work.

REMOVING ENERGY BLOCKAGES

An important part of the process of removing energy blocks is to become aware of our conditioned reactions and characteristic patterns and make a commitment to practices that can lead us from the bondage of tedious, repetitive thought processes, emotional habits, and self-defeating behaviors to true freedom. Meditation, yoga, chakra/Kundalini practices, pranayama, chanting/mantra repetition, devotion, and selfless service are all applied systems of self-transformation, developed over thousands of years and proven successful for centuries. In this book you will be given examples of these practices and shown how to apply them in order to unblock your energies.

PRACTICE NOTE FOR CHAKRA WORK

Maintain a Daily Practice Workbook Journal for the duration of your chakra work. Use it to record your experiences of each practice. It is an important tool for review at intervals. After each notation in this journal, move on. Every three to four weeks or so, it is helpful to review what you have written. However, don't dwell on anything—the process takes its own momentum. Just reflect on your responses, experiences, and changes, which reflect your unfolding.

Continue with the practices for each chakra until you feel clear in this center. Chakra clearing work is done sequentially, and you will discover that there is a natural impulse to move to the next ascending chakra when the preceding one is clear. Apply honesty and clarity to ensure the impulse to move on does not arise out of boredom or restlessness—this often occurs. There is little to gain and more to lose in doing your spiritual practices piecemeal or on an ad hoc basis. All effective spiritual practices are systematic in their approach. It is far more effective to commit fully to one meditation practice daily, along with observance of the moral precepts, or ethical living, for as long as it takes to attain your goal.

The minimum practice requirements for this chakra clearing work are the mantra practices and yantra meditations/visualizations, along with maintaining your Workbook Journal and ethical living practices.

PRACTICE ROUTINE

The goal of chakra work is to follow the path toward Self-realization. This path involves meditation, sound/mantra and visualization practices, some physical exercises, and contemplative Self-inquiry. These practices will enable you to purify all levels of being, which is essential preparation for the awakening of the spiritualizing energy of the Kundalini Shakti. When you are working on the chakras, the intermediate goal is to render them inactive by arousing the ascending flow of the Kundalini Shakti energy through the chakra. The final result of the chakra work or Tantra Yoga practices frees a person from all effects of the chakras.

SEQUENCE FOR PRACTICES

In traditional chakra practices, particular sequences are adhered to in the meditations, chanting, and visualizations of each chakra. Generally, the practices are done gradually and the sequence is as follows:

1. Meditating on the lotus petals and chanting the syllables inscribed on the petals.
2. Meditation and visualization of the yantra of the chakra and the vehicle or animal carrier of the seed sound, the bija mantra.
3. Chanting the seed sound.
4. Meditation on the Shakti, the *Devi,* and form of Kundalini in each chakra, then the *Deva,* the male deity of the chakra.

Illustrations will help when you meditate upon the deities of a chakra. Use the illustrations in this book and traditional pictures of Indian deities or pictographs of the chakras—which include all the symbolic aspects of a chakra—now widely available in books, on the Internet, and in stores carrying Indian merchandise. You can also meditate on your preferred form of Creator deity according to your chosen spiritual tradition—for example, Buddha or Christ for the Devas (male forms) and Tara, Kuan Yin, or the Mother of Christ for the Devis (female forms). Include male and female forms, as a goal of this work is the union of polarities, and meditate and reflect upon the symbolic meanings of the implements held by the governing deities for each chakra. (See Chapters Four to Ten.)

MORE ABOUT CHAKRA PRACTICES

Committed practitioners do these practices in conjunction with various asanas, pranayama practices, and mudras (symbolic gestures). To pursue this path in greater depth, in addition to working with the chakra practices outlined here, it is advisable to consult an accomplished teacher. If your time is limited, to simplify the practice routine you could follow the meditative and yoga chakra awakening practices, mantra, and yantra meditations/visualizations. Whatever you decide, apply patience, flexibility, commitment, time, and routine practice, setting aside a regular time each day.

Traditional chakra practices, unlike many of those adopted in the West, do not focus on a particular physical point of the body, or the gross organs, said to be related to particular chakras. This is because the chakras are located in the subtle body and not in the physical body. Hence the chakras are indirectly, rather than directly, related to particular body areas that house specific body organs. There are yoga practices for awakening the chakras, such as those included in this book, which focus on a chakra at the same time as working on the physical areas related to that chakra.

Meditation is at the heart of these practices and finding a suitably comfortable posture where you can maintain an erect spine and stillness of the body is essential. This will be covered in individual practices later in this book. (Also see pages 44–45.)

SEQUENCE FOR CHAKRAS

Meditations and visualizations on the chakras are usually done in sequence from the first chakra to the seventh. However, some yoga schools advocate working initially on the awakening of the **Ajna** chakra, the sixth chakra (see Chapter Nine), then working sequentially from the first chakra upward. With the opening of the "third eye" related to the Ajna chakra, we can gain more insight when dealing with the energies of the other chakras and may be more able to manage powerful energies awakened through Kundalini yoga practices and chakra work. This book adopts this approach.

MANAGING CHANGE

Taking up any spiritual path means change—which the ego invariably and tenaciously resists. Change is a subtle process, which is always occurring even if not apparent on the surface, so patience is required when progress seems slow. Change can also come in seemingly sudden eruptions that require clear decisions in line with your overall purpose in life. The practices outlined in this book are designed to stabilize and heal the body–mind to better withstand the overall changes that accompany transformations. In time you will also learn to trust the process of higher guidance.

WORKBOOK EXERCISES

1. Read the following statement, and then note how you think the fears in your life have blocked your energies:

   "Fear is perhaps one of the greatest obstacles to be overcome if we desire to be healthy and ultimately free. It can alert us to physical danger of harm or pain, but when it enters our psychological being, we begin to contract—to suppress, to deny, to evade. These are all ways of subverting and blocking the natural free-flow of energy."

2. Make a list of three of your most **prevalent fears.** Now list your reactions to these fears. Rate each of these fears on a scale of one to ten—one being least, ten being most—in their severity and impact on your life.

3. Make a list of three of your **deepest fears.** Write down three ways you are currently dealing with these fears and three ways they are subtly influencing your life. List your immediate reactions—thoughts, sensations, and emotions associated with these fears. Now list five possible strategies for better dealing with these fears in the future.

4. Reflect, at the end of a day, on some of the repetitive and self-defeating thoughts, emotions, and behaviors you experienced that day. List three of these. Now list which of these are the most repetitive and/or the most debilitating in your life. Are there any other such thoughts, emotions, and behaviors you have observed in yourself? List a minimum of three ways that these have affected your health, your relationships, and your sense of well-being and happiness.

A CAUTIONARY NOTE ON AWAKENING KUNDALINI

The aim of chakra work is to arouse the spiritualizing energy of the Kundalini Shakti. As discussed, the human system needs preparation and purification to clear the pathway for Kundalini and to withstand the powerful upsurge of her energy.

Have the highest respect for the powerful Shakti Energy and systematically purify and clear your system so that you are prepared for the transformational Kundalini Shakti if and when she does awaken.

BASIC YOGA POSTURES FOR MEDITATION

For all yoga practices, pranayama, and meditations, wear loose clothing, preferably of natural fiber. For sitting postures, use a low cushion under the buttocks. The spine must always be kept straight. Perform all practices in a warm, well-ventilated but not drafty room. Practices need to be done on an empty stomach. Early morning is the best time for practices. Other suitable times are dusk and last thing at night.

1. *Sukha asana*—**Easy posture** The easiest sitting meditation posture. Before crossing legs for any posture, sit with legs extended and bend one leg into position, then the other. Also, alternate the leg placed on top so that muscle stretch and flexibility remain equal. Rest hands either on the knees with palms up and the tip of the thumb and index fingers touching, or rest hands in lap, palms up with the right hand inside the left.

2. *Siddha asana* and *Siddha yoni asana*—**Male accomplished posture and Female accomplished posture** The best posture for chakra-awakening yoga practices and meditations. Follow the procedures outlined for sukha asana; however, when folding the legs, place the sole of one foot flat against the inside of the thigh of the other leg. **Men**: press the heel against the perineum—between the anus and the genitals. **Women**: press the heel against the labia majora. Place the foot of the upper leg on the calf of the underside leg, with the toes in the space between the calf and thigh.

3. *Padma asana*—Lotus pose After extending legs forward, bend one leg and place the foot on top of the opposite thigh, with the sole upward and the heel touching the pelvic bone. Bend the other leg and place the foot in a similar position on the other thigh. If needed, place a foam or wooden block under the knees for support.

Note: Do not practice siddha asana, siddha yoni asana, or padma asana if you are suffering from lower-back disorders.

Pranayama is a system of Hatha Yoga breathing practices to control and direct the flow of prana in the body. Pranayama exercises are generally performed after asana practice and before meditation. Generally speaking, pranayama is an advanced set of practices that need to be learned from an experienced yoga teacher. They require adherence to correct procedure so as not to do any damage. This aligns with ***ahimsa***, the first principle of yoga— "to do no harm." However, there are a couple of basic practices beneficial to all, and helpful for meditation. One of these practices is ***nadi shodan*** (alternate nostril breathing—a pranayama practice from Hatha Yoga to purify the nadis, see page 46).

PRANAYAMA: NADI SHODAN EXERCISE

Pranayama needs to be performed with an empty stomach—it is best performed in the early morning before breakfast. An alternate time is last thing at night (three to four hours after meals). Pranayama is usually practiced after yoga asanas or physical relaxation exercises and before meditation practices. In this book, pranayama is used after chakra awakening practices and before meditations. Wash the hands, face, and feet before starting.

Sit in any comfortable meditation posture. Keep the spine, neck, and head upright and aligned. Relax the whole body and close the eyes. For a few minutes, practice breathing from the abdomen to the chest to the collarbone on the inhalation, and without pause, reverse the path on the exhalation (known as the Yogic Breath). This is an excellent breathing practice in itself.

Rest the hands on the knees. With the right hand:
1. Place the fingers of the right hand in front of the face.
2. Rest the index and middle fingers gently between the eyebrows. Both fingers should be relaxed.
3. With the thumb, close the right nostril, blocking the air flow. The ring finger should rest adjacent to the left nostril.
4. Breathing naturally, inhale and exhale five times through the left nostril. Be aware of each breath.
5. After five breaths, release the thumb pressure on the right nostril and press the left nostril with the ring finger.
6. Breathing normally, inhale and exhale five times through the right nostril.
7. Lower the hand to your knee and breathe five times through both nostrils.

This constitutes one round. Practice five rounds or for five minutes, ensuring there is no sound as the air passes through the nostrils. Maintain a relaxed, slow, and steady pace.

Try to practice this each day for at least fifteen days.

MEDITATIONS, VISUALIZATIONS, AND SOUND PRACTICES

The following meditations, visualizations, and exercises can help to transform the undesirable negative qualities associated with unbalanced or blocked energy in a chakra. Before commencing with them, follow the simple relaxation breathing exercise (page 48) and the simple pranayama practice (page 49) for ten days to two weeks, and notice if you feel any different. For example, do you feel more relaxed? Less stressed? Calmer yet more alert?

MEDITATIONS

Commence the chakra work by following the awakening practice for each chakra. Then add the first sound meditation practice. Stay with this meditation practice for a while until there is a natural inclination to progress to the next practice. It is best to stay with one practice before commencing the next so you can monitor the effects of each practice on your system. You can then combine these practices:

- meditation and mantra
- pranayama and meditation
- pranayama, meditation, and mantra
- asanas, pranayama, mantra, meditation and/or visualization

When you have incorporated all the practices for a chakra and when you feel clear in that chakra, then move on to work on the next chakra. Follow this method throughout the book.

When you are working with a particular chakra, use only the practices suggested for that chakra. Do not mix and match, as this will nullify the benefits and could even prove harmful. Avoid changing practices out of boredom or if challenges are emerging—instead stay with these and see what they have to reveal.

For those who are new to meditation or who want to vary their existing practice routine, the simple relaxation breathing exercise (page 48) and simple pranayama practice (page 49) can be done prior to beginning a meditation, mantra/sound practice, or visualization. These practices are alternative practices to nadi shodan (page 46).

Use these breathing practices after you have set up your meditation space for a particular meditation, and once you are sitting in meditation posture. You can effectively incorporate these practices into all of your routine meditations.

SIMPLE RELAXATION BREATHING EXERCISE

This is a simple yet very effective exercise using the breath to relax the body. The body–mind follows the breath and vice-versa.

1. Sit in meditation posture—sukha asana, siddha asana, or siddha yoni asana—on a meditation stool or on a chair with your spine straight and feet resting on the ground. Do not lean against the back of the chair. Hold yourself erect.
2. Place hands in lap, left hand cradling right hand with palms facing upward.
3. Breathing naturally, inhale to the count of four or five and exhale to the count of four or five (4:4 or 5:5).
4. Consciously relax the body on the out breath.
5. Scan your body and note any tension areas. Breathe into those areas on the in breaths and relax them on the out breaths.
6. Continue for a few minutes.
7. Repeat this pattern for a few minutes until the body feels relaxed.
8. Begin the meditation or visualization.

As well as acting as a prelude to meditation practices, this exercise can be done any time you feel tense. This exercise can be extended, through practice, to the simple pranayama practice (page 49) that follows to be done prior to meditations, mantra repetition, and visualizations.

SIMPLE PRANAYAMA PRACTICE

1. Begin with the simple relaxation breathing exercise (page 48). Inhale to the count of four and exhale to the count of four (4:4). Repeat four times.
2. Now inhale to the count of four and exhale to the count of eight. Repeat four times.
3. Now inhale to the count of four, hold the breath to the count of four, exhale to the count of eight, and hold the breath to the count of four. Repeat four times. When you have become familiar with this breathing pattern, do this segment as a stand-alone practice prior to meditations, mantra repetitions, and visualizations. In this case, repeat at least five times or in increments of five.
4. Next, inhale to the count of four, hold to the count of eight, exhale to the count of eight, and hold to the count of four.
5. Inhale to the count of four, hold to the count of eight, exhale to the count of eight, hold to the count of eight. Repeat four times.

This entire practice, once familiar, takes approximately seven to eight minutes. It can also be done incorporating a *jalandhara bandha* (chin lock)—see Chapter Five, page 77, for a description—which increases its effectiveness.

WORKBOOK EXERCISES

1. Note three aspects that you found easiest/most enjoyable and three aspects you found the most difficult about the simple relaxation breathing exercise on the first day of practice. Answer these questions again after ten days of daily practice. What changes did you notice?
2. Repeat the exercise above with the simple pranayama practice, except do this practice for two weeks. Compare your written responses at the beginning of the practice and after the two weeks of daily practice.

CHAPTER FOUR

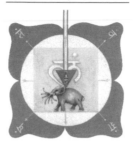

THE MULADHARA CHAKRA

Learn about the first, or root, chakra and its characteristics. Where is the first chakra located? Learn how to awaken the first chakra through meditations on sound, mantra, yantra, and its deities.

Muladhara is the first, or root, chakra. Muladhara is from the Sanskrit *mula* (root) and *adhara* (support). The Muladhara chakra is the seat of consciousness and the Kundalini Shakti, and the location of unconscious powers.

Location In the perineum—between the anus and the genitals, at the base of the spine.

Tattwa/Element Earth. Color: yellow.

Color Red.

Lotus Blood red, with four petals. The petals signify the four directions, the four corners of the world. They also signify the four levels of bliss or modes of our being maintained by sense functioning, as this is the base of immensely pleasurable sensation. These four sensate levels are:

- pure joy
- natural pleasure
- satisfaction in controlling the desires
- meditative bliss

Blood is life and life is precious, and all forms of life are to be revered as manifestations of the One reality—that is, they should be revered as Oneself. Life is an opportunity to evolve and to awaken to our own essential Divinity.

Letters on the Lotus Petals Vam, sam, sam, sam. (The letters are written in this book without their Sanskrit accents.) Letters are symbols of sound vibration.

Seed Sound/Bija Mantra Lam—symbol for awakening consciousness.

Vehicle of the Seed Sound The elephant Airavata, the vehicle of Indra, the Vedic lord of the celestial beings. It symbolizes the strength and solidity of the earth, as well as the qualities of endurance, abundance, memory, steadfastness, and longevity. Its color— white—symbolizes the inherently spiritual nature of being. Airavata has seven trunks, representing the seven constituents of the physical body: earth/clay; blood; fluids; bones; bone marrow; flesh; and fat. These also represent the seven colors of the rainbow created by refracted clear light, the notes of the octave, the seven chakras, and the seven major planets. Seven has long been considered a mystical number.

Associated Female Deity Shakti Dakini.

Associated Male Deity Child Brahma.

Associated Sense Smell.

Sense Organ The nose.

Associated Plexus and Glands The sacro-coccygeal nerve plexus, the testes, and ovaries. The "work organ" is the anus.

Associated Parts of the Body Spinal column; the bones; the immune system; the lower limbs—legs; feet.

Ruling Planet Mars.

Associated Astrological Signs and Planets in Western Astrology: Aries and Mars; Capricorn and Saturn; Taurus and Venus.

CHARACTERISTICS

The Muladhara chakra represents the first stage of human development, as well as the first developmental stage in human evolution. It is the seat of consciousness, the boundary between animal and human consciousness, and the location of the unconscious.

This chakra encompasses the energies that dominate growth from infancy to seven years of age. This period represents early family experiences, the influences of our "tribe" or cultural group, and the aspect of security. The Muladhara chakra also holds our tendencies and karmas from previous lives. The energy of the element earth is associated with this chakra, and the element earth is also associated with the mother. The mother gives birth to us, feeds and nurtures us, protects and cares for us—to a certain degree, because we have our own characteristics, inclinations, karma, and our own destiny, for which we are responsible. We are also responsible to the mother, the Earth, who physically sustains us. In Tantra Yoga it is the Divine Mother, the Kundalini Shakti, who gives birth to, or reawakens, our spiritual consciousness.

The manifestation and development of human consciousness proceeds from the Muladhara chakra upward. This suggests that we move up and away from earthly attachments, concerns, negativities, and karmas, represented by the first three chakras, toward the higher powers latent in the upper four chakras. The Muladhara chakra is the seat of the coiled Kundalini Shakti and is the root of growth and awakening to the awareness of the Divinity that is our true nature. However, when the energy of this chakra is blocked, preventing energy from flowing into the higher centers, the energy can become perverted, making a person egocentric and harmful to others.

Negative and undesirable qualities associated with the lower chakras disappear when Kundalini Shakti rises above them. As we reach the higher chakras, the qualities become increasingly positive, transforming darkness into light.

OPERATING ON THE PHYSICAL PLANE

The Muladhara chakra operates on the physical plane of existence. It is the center of our base instincts for survival, self-preservation, and security. Those strongly influenced by first-chakra concerns have a great need to feel safe, and will feel secure only when their basic physical and financial needs are met. They are conservative, law-abiding, and hierarchical in organizational approach. They can be servile to those "above them," but tough on those whom they perceive to be "below them," or with whom they are in competition. They work hard to satisfy their driving need for stability, housing, food, and security. They usually have hardy constitutions, dogged dispositions, and considerable endurance. They may be unsure of their direction in life and seek the approval and advice of others.

ENERGY BLOCKAGES

This chakra influences the spine, nervous system, blood, bones, vagina, testes, rectum, and immune system. Unbalanced or blocked Muladhara chakra energies can manifest as single or multiple disorders that indicate either a deficiency or excess of energy in this center.

PHYSICAL DISORDERS

Physical disorders may include spinal and other back problems, particularly in the lower back; leg problems; vaginal or testicular disorders; constipation; hemorrhoids; obesity; and problems related to the immune system.

PSYCHOLOGICAL DISORDERS

These may include primal fears of death, annihilation, abandonment, chaos, humiliation, intimacy, or physical or psychological harm. Other problems are lethargy, lack of confidence, worry, anxiety, depression, too little or too much willpower, addictive behavior, compulsiveness, obsessiveness, domineering personality, egocentricity, extreme selfishness, rigidity, tunnel vision, workaholism driven by low self-worth and hunger for recognition, illusion, delusion, anger, hostility, aggression, lack of confidence, greed, and sexual inhibitions or perversions.

TRANSCENDING THE MULADHARA CHAKRA

In order to transcend this chakra, we must endeavor to move beyond our preoccupation with survival and our identification with the physical body. This means a willingness to face and address our unresolved issues relating to our families, our early experiences, our overall health, security issues, and matters of trust.

We need to be willing to review our foundations in life and examine our underlying attitudes to the world, to relationships, and to Divinity. This can allow the fear of death or extinction to vanish as we come to realize that we are not the physical body but are of the immortal Spirit; though our state of being may change, we can never actually die—only the physical body dies.

BALANCING THE ENERGIES

When the Muladhara chakra energies are balanced or unblocked, this can manifest as greater physical vitality and a sense of well-being. A heavy, serious, and unbalanced attitude to life gives way to a more relaxed, lighter sense of being, with a renewed interest in healthier and more balanced ways of living. We feel more grounded and more in control of our drive and life direction. This extends to allowing ourselves to be more authentic, open, and vulnerable, instead of defensive and suspicious; we become more comfortable with emotional expression. We then gain more readiness to accept, rather than resent, the seeming adversities of life and learn what we need to learn from them.

WORKBOOK EXERCISES

Read carefully through the characteristics section again and write down your responses—as honestly as you can and without censorship—to the following questions in your Workbook Journal.

1. The Muladhara chakra is the center of our instincts for survival, self-preservation, and security. Write down five things you associate with: survival—physical and psychological; chaos; order; self-preservation; and feeling physically and emotionally safe.

2. In response to your answers to each of the above questions, write down three ways that your beliefs assist you in life and three ways they may obstruct your psychological growth.

3. Rate on a score of one to ten—one being the least, ten being the most—how you see your overall health.

4. List five associations you have with pain.

5. Note the physical areas and disorders associated with this chakra and list any discomforts or ailments in any of these areas. With each one, note when you first noticed an ongoing discomfort and what you did in response. Has the discomfort/disorder increased or lessened, or does it come and go? What are your thoughts/beliefs and actions in relation to the disorder/s?

6. How do you react to the beliefs/values/opinions of others when they differ from your own? List four reactions.

7. List the three most humiliating things you can imagine happening to you.

8. Write down your greatest concerns/fears regarding death.

9. Do you need the approval of others? Rate yourself on a scale of one to ten.

10. Do you worry a lot in your life? What are your principal concerns—number them in order from one to eight.

11. What makes you angry? What do you do with your anger? Make a list.

12. Make a list of your six most important ambitions in life.

AWAKENING THE CHAKRAS

We do not know what will emerge when we awaken each chakra. Powerful karmic energies, both active and inactive, are housed in both the Muladhara and Svadisthana chakras, and this needs to be taken into account when awakening these chakras. All past impressions from this life and previous lives are buried in the Muladhara chakra. When the Kundalini Shakti is awakened and begins to ascend, both active and inactive karma are unleashed. These energies then flood the consciousness of an individual. For some, the emotional, physical, and mental changes this triggers can be overwhelming. For many, the awakened Kundalini Shakti just retreats back to the Muladhara chakra because of karmic energy blocks.

As suggested earlier, to overcome this obstacle, it is preferable to concentrate on awakening the Ajna chakra, the sixth chakra, before any of the other chakras. Doing so will enable you to purify the karma of the lower chakras. In addition, if you initially activate the Ajna chakra, the Kundalini Shakti will be stimulated because of the direct connection between the Ajna and Muladhara chakras.

Therefore, it is advisable to go to Chapter Nine and follow the practice instructions for awakening, clearing, and harmonizing the Ajna Chakra. When this chakra is awakened and cleansed, come back and work more on the Muladhara chakra and the ascending chakras in sequence. As you work to unblock and purify each chakra, what is unresolved will come to light to be released.

It is very important to stay grounded during energy clearing work (see the hara breathing exercise in Chapter Eleven, page 178). It is also advisable to read this book straight through before beginning your chakra work to gain a good conceptual understanding of this path.

MEDITATION FOR AWAKENING THE MULADHARA CHAKRA

Meditations for this chakra are assisted by being in the presence of earth, the related element of this chakra. Place a handful of earth in a container nearby, sit near the presence of Mother Earth or sit outdoors either on or close to the ground. It is said that this assists the meditation and helps the meditator in developing good health, intellectual ability, physical strength, and longevity.

A highly regarded traditional meditation used in the awakening of all the chakras—in conjunction with other techniques—comes from a treatise written in the tenth century. This is a process of meditating on the tip of the nose while concentrating on the symbols and meanings of a particular chakra as represented in the chakra diagrams, rather than on any physical location in the body. However, there are yoga practices for awakening and clearing the chakras that incorporate a focus on the physical area related to those chakras. Some will be covered in this book.

This meditation practice is in two parts. It is recommended that you practice the first part for at least a week, particularly if you are not used to meditation. After this and/or when you feel comfortable, incorporate the second stage. Then do the entire practice as your regular meditation for awakening the Muladhara chakra. As mentioned earlier, it is also recommended that you first practice awakening the Ajna chakra, the sixth chakra.

NOTES ON THE MEDITATION

It is said that this meditation for awakening the Muladhara chakra, when practiced regularly, induces awareness, increases vitality, endurance, stability, security, and well-being, and bestows freedom from the darkness of ignorance.

The main obstacle is the very simplicity that makes this meditation effective. To the beginner it may become monotonous, allowing for easy distraction by thoughts and desires emerging from the subconscious and resulting in fractured concentration and a restless mind. For these reasons, Tantra Yoga has devised other effective practices for awakening the chakras. Basically, these combine the above chakra concentration meditation with pranayama, asanas, and mudras. The combined practices are for committed yoga practitioners and need to be learned under the guidance of an experienced and skilled yoga teacher. However, anyone can follow this chakra meditation practice. It is an excellent practice for developing concentration, as well as for awakening the chakras. All that it requires is a quiet place, a set time, your attention, and commitment to regular practice.

AWAKENING MULADHARA: PART ONE

Adopt your meditation posture—sukha asana, siddha asana, or siddha yoni asana—or sit on a meditation stool or chair if asanas are difficult. As with all sitting meditations, maintain a still and relaxed body. Keep the spine straight and neck and head aligned.

1. Practice a few minutes of simple relaxation breathing (page 48), then continue to breathe naturally.
2. Close your eyes and direct your inward gaze to the tip of your nose. When you have located it, you will feel a sensation at the tip of the nose. Concentrate your gaze here.
3. Now open your eyes slightly, ensuring your surrounding eye muscles are relaxed, and keep your gaze fixed on the same point. Disregard the fact that you may not be able to see the tip of your nose, but you may continue to feel a sensation in that area.
4. When the eyes feel tired, close them for a little while. When they are rested, open them again and resume gazing as before.
5. Repeat this process for ten to twenty minutes.

AWAKENING MULADHARA: PART TWO

Now direct your attention to the perineum. Alternately, contract and relax the perineum for about ten minutes. As you become accustomed to this practice, try to increase the time in increments of five minutes to about twenty minutes—and longer if you can.

EFFECTS OF THE MEDITATION

Although this meditation is simple, when practiced regularly it is highly effective at awakening the Muladhara chakra, for a number of reasons:

- The nose is the sense organ of the Muladhara chakra and the seat of the major nadis. Through the nose the breath enters and departs from the physical body.
- It is through the breath that prana, the vital life force, enters the body.
- The nose is also the termination point of the Ida Nadi (left nostril) and the Pingala Nadi (right nostril)—which originate in the Muladhara chakra.

SOUND

Here is an exercise for intoning the Sanskrit letters **vam, sam, sam, sam** inscribed on the four lotus petals. These are pronounced **vang, shang, kshang, sang.**

The inscriptions on the petals signify that every sound and every word has an inherent power. This power is connected to all aspects of being—physical, emotional, mental, and the highest dimensions of Spirit.

This practice is similar to the sound meditation and mantra practice of intoning the bija mantra **lam** (see page 60). First practice this meditation by itself in sitting meditation. This way you can become accustomed to the practice and also note its subtle effects over a period of time—say, four to six weeks to begin. When you become accustomed to the practice, you can combine it with a visualization practice, which also needs to be done on its own in the beginning. You need to acclimatize yourself to any one practice before combining it with another practice.

SOUND MEDITATION

Decide on a definite time for the sound meditation practice—say five to ten minutes in the early stages of the practice. Adopt your meditation posture. Practice a few minutes of simple relaxation breathing (page 48) or simple pranayama practice (page 49) for five rounds. Intone **vang, shang, kshang, sang** out loud continuously for the duration of the meditation. At the end of your meditation, sit quietly for a few minutes; notice the silence and the energy in and around your body.

Note the effects of your meditation in your Workbook Journal.

Cautionary note: If you start to feel dizzy or become breathless while doing the sound meditations, simply resume normal breathing. This is quite a common bodily reaction when beginning these practices. As your lungs and body become accustomed to the increase of oxygen and infusion of energy, the symptoms will usually disappear.

SOUND MEDITATION—MANTRA

In this meditation you intone **lam,** the bija mantra of the lotus Muladhara.

The pronunciation of **lam** is **lang.** *La* is connected to the element earth and *ng* is the nada-bindu—primal cosmic sound—out of which the universe manifested. If you elect to do one mantra practice, then focus on this practice. It is similar, but not identical, to intoning the letters on the petals of the lotus (see page 59). First practice this meditation on its own in sitting meditation to acclimatize—again, for four to six weeks to begin. Later you can combine it with a visualization practice; also initially do this on its own for four to six weeks.

SOUND MEDITATION—MANTRA

Decide on a definite time for the meditation. In the beginning stages, start with five to ten minutes. Adopt your meditation posture. Practice a few minutes of simple relaxation breathing (page 48) or simple pranayama practice (page 49) for five rounds.

Form the sound **lang** by placing the lips in a squarish shape and pushing the tongue against the palate. Intone the mantra on the note of middle C; if this is not comfortable, find your preferred note and maintain that pitch.

Inhale deeply, and on the exhalation begin to intone **la-ng** out loud. The sound vibrates the palate, the brain, and the top of the cranium. Follow this pattern for the duration of the meditation.

At the end of your meditation, sit quietly for a few minutes; notice the silence and the energy in and around your body.

Note the effects of your meditation in your Workbook Journal.

YANTRA

The square—geometric symbol of the earth principle—represents the Earth itself, the four directions, and the four dimensions—often surrounded by eight spears, which are directed toward the eight points of the compass. The seat of the bija mantra, it can release sound in all of the eight directional points. The square is yellow and surrounded by the lotus circle. At the center is a bright red, downward-pointing triangle also known as **tripura,** meaning "three worlds." These are the three aspects of consciousness, the three modes of experience, and the Hindu Trinity—Brahma, Vishnu, and Shiva.

The triangle is also called the **Yoni**—the symbol for the female sex organ, the vagina—an abode of creative and generative power, and a seat of desire. This is the seat of the Kundalini Shakti, representing feminine energy, curled three and a half times around the **Svayambu Lingam**—symbol of the male sex organ, the phallus, and representing masculine energy. *Svayambu* means "self-originated" and *Ling* "gender," and represents the masculine energetic principle. It is also symbolic of the deity Shiva, the third principle in the Hindu Trinity.

Kundalini Shakti covers the entrance to the Sushumna Nadi with her mouth. The three and a half coils represent the three **gunas** (qualities) of energy:

- **sattva**—purity, lightness, balance, and clarity
- **rajas**—passion and activity
- **tamas**—inertia and darkness

The half coil is said to combine the three qualities and represent their interplay. This area is also the originating point of numerous nadis, including the major ones—Sushumna (and the Brahma Nadi), Vajrini, Chitrini, Ida, and Pingala. Kundalini Shakti and the Svayambu Lingam—female and male, hot and cool, moonlike and sunlike respectively—represent the eternal pairing of polarities. The union of these polarities in spiritual awakening is the goal of chakra and Kundalini work or Tantra Yoga.

YANTRA MEDITATION AND VISUALIZATION

When practicing this meditation, try to have some earth nearby to enhance your meditation. Place a picture of the yantra (see Figure 1) where you can easily see it without any strain while keeping your head, neck, and spine in alignment. Adopt your preferred meditation posture.

Practice a few minutes of simple relaxation breathing (page 48) to relax your body–mind.

Begin the meditation by first focusing on the lotus petals surrounding the yantra for a few minutes (see page 61 for a review of the lotus symbol). Now focus on the square of the yantra, which represents earth.

When you gaze at the square, reflect on the properties of earth and its symbolic associations (described on page 52). Remain open to the images, insights, and intuitions that may arise. The yellow color of the yantra is associated with the intellect; it is also an optimistic and uplifting color. The energy of the color is to help illuminate the intellect to take it beyond the rational and analytical to higher levels of consciousness. Absorb the ambience of the color.

Next, focus on the downward pointing red triangle that symbolizes feminine energy. Remember, this is the seat of the Divine Mother Energy, the Kundalini Shakti. Reflect on the symbolism of the triangle and how this manifests in your life. Reflect also on masculine energy—represented by the Svayambu Lingam in the triangle—and how you see the polarities of feminine and masculine energy expressing themselves in your life.

Like the thoughts that arise in meditation, you may notice what arises. Let it all pass rather than allowing your concentration to fragment. Remain internally detached and remain singly focused on the object of the meditation. If you do become distracted or caught in a net of thoughts, simply bring yourself back to the concentration point of the yantra.

Note the effects of your meditation in your Workbook Journal.

WORKBOOK EXERCISES

1. At the beginning of the yantra meditation and visualization, you may pose a question related to the element earth when gazing at the square or one related to the feminine and masculine aspects of energy and/or the aspect of Divine Creation when gazing at the triangle inside the square. However, the process is not one of analytical thought but rather one of staying open to whatever arises. Note your experiences of this practice in your Workbook Journal.

2. Also reflect on the following and write down your responses in your Workbook Journal:
   • Write down five qualities you associate with Mother Earth and with earth itself.
   • Write down five thoughts/feelings you have about being on Earth and their meaning to you.
   • Do you feel grounded in your body? List at least four ways that this manifests.
   • List five ways you do/do not feel grounded in your life.

3. All human beings are constituted of feminine and masculine energy—irrespective of sex. Although these energies are always present, sometimes one or the other—or a blend—is prominent at different times and on different occasions in our lives.
   • Write down six qualities you associate with feminine energy. List how these qualities manifest in your life and rate each one on a scale of one to ten as you experience it now.
   • Write down six qualities you associate with masculine energy. List how these qualities manifest in your life and rate each one on a scale of one to ten as you experience it now.
   • Which energies appear strongest in your life now? Write down what, if anything, this means to you.

4. Continue to note your experiences of this practice in your Workbook Journal.

DEITIES

ASSOCIATED FEMALE DEITY (FORM OF KUNDALINI): SHAKTI DAKINI

Dakini signifies the feminine aspect of Energy unmanifest. Dakini is the presiding Divinity, the *Shakti*—the Power or Energy—of the Muladhara chakra, and the keeper of the door or entrance to the Sushumna Nadi. Dakini is depicted as radiant, brilliant, and a bearer of abundance, and usually described as bright red, with red eyes. She carries the light of Divine knowledge, which she reveals to those adept at meditating upon her. Her single head denotes one-pointed concentration in which the ego, or "I-consciousness," dissolves.

Dakini has four arms and hands. One hand carries a spear, which is said to destroy those animal instincts that hinder awareness in order to remove fear, destroy ignorance, and assist the aspirant in overcoming all difficulties and obstacles. (In some iconographies this hand holds a trident—symbol of the energies of the Hindu Trinity.) Another hand holds a skull, or staff with a skull, which symbolizes detachment from the fear of death or annihilation, from worldly passions, and from material attachments. The skull can also indicate the "clear head"—empty of the ego or conditioned thought—through which Divine intuition and insight can be received through the flow of life-force energy rising in the staff (the spine, Sushumna Nadi). She also holds a sword, a symbol of discrimination. Learning to discriminate is an essential quality to develop right at the beginning of the spiritual path, and will enable us to "sort the seeds" of the real from the fanciful or erroneous, and the necessary from the unnecessary. It also helps us to quickly correct the errors, misjudgments, distractions, negative habits, and attachments that ordinarily beset the seeker's path. The sword also represents destruction of ignorance and fear, as well as protection. Dakini also holds a cup of wine; wine symbolizes Spirit, the "Nectar of Bliss," which awaits those who steadfastly hold to the path and overcome the various hazards and obstacles along the way.

MEDITATION ON SHAKTI DAKINI

As with other meditations for the Muladhara chakra, you should have the element earth nearby. Reflect on the symbolic meanings of the implements that are held by the governing deities—even if you have chosen your own deities. Alternatively, focus on the element and the yantra associated with each chakra and the sound practices/mantra repetition (which are simple cleansing and clearing vibrational practices), and contemplate the characteristic qualities of each chakra.

Decide on a time for your meditation. Try to allow at least fifteen to twenty minutes to begin with—including relaxation time and notation time at the end. Adopt meditation posture sukha asana, siddha asana, or siddha yoni asana for yoga practitioners, and sukha asana (easy posture) or other sitting position—either on a floor cushion or a chair—for others. Do not lean against the chair back. Ensure your body is relaxed and comfortable and your spine straight.

Assume meditation posture. Begin the practice with five minutes of simple relaxation breathing (page 48) or simple pranayama practice (page 49) for five rounds. With concentrated but relaxed attention, focus on an image of Shakti Dakini as the creative power of Brahma, in her radiant, rather than fiery, state. Alternatively, meditate on a picture of your chosen Devi or female deity. At the end of your meditation, allow yourself to sit quietly for a few minutes.

Note the effects of your meditation in your Workbook Journal.

ASSOCIATED MALE DEITY: CHILD BRAHMA

Brahma is the God of Creation, the first principle in the *Trimurti*, the Hindu Trinity. In the first chakra, Brahma signifies the masculine aspect of Divine Energy unmanifest. He has four heads and four arms. Each head represents one of the four dimensions of human consciousness:

- the physical **body–mind** self—the cellular body and its consciousness
- the **rational** self—the conditioned reasoning or intellectual aspect
- the **emotional** self—the various fluctuating moods and emotions within an individual
- the **intuitive** self—the inner voice of the conscious mind

The four heads also represent the four Vedas in which Brahma has revealed Divine universal wisdom. The four arms and four heads represent the four forms of sound:

- unmanifest
- manifested as primal vibrations
- organized or defined sounds with tone such as the voice
- intelligibly sounded communication

Brahma is the dispeller of fears and insecurities. He carries a blessing or "boon" for the seeker in each hand. He holds a staff—symbolic of the spine supporting the body. Prana maintains the levels of consciousness and is dominant in the spine. The staff also signifies support, fearlessness, and beneficence. In some iconographies this hand carries scrolls signifying Divine wisdom. Brahma also holds a gourd or water pot to quench thirst, or an elixir (sacred healing water), or a lotus flower, and a *mala* (rosary) to assist in **mantra japa** (mantra recitation). The remaining hand is in a mudra to dispel fear where there is sincere good intent.

MEDITATION ON BRAHMA

The best times for this meditation are during the twilight hours of dawn and dusk, when the energy is calm, pure, and clear—like that of Brahma. The preliminaries are the same as for the meditation on Shakti Dakini—see page 65. Decide on a specific time for your meditation.

Breathe naturally. Begin with a few minutes of simple relaxation breathing exercise (page 48) or simple pranayama practice (page 49). Begin your meditation practice by simply focusing on a picture of Brahma (or your chosen Deva or male deity). Doing so evokes a calm stillness and clarity of mind. When you are familiar with an image of Brahma, instead of focusing on a picture, try to invoke his presence in your mind's eye. Be aware of Brahma's symbolic meaning—the Creator aspect of the Hindu Trinity—as well as the symbology of the implements he holds (see page 66). When your attention wanders, bring yourself back to the subject of your meditation. At the end of your meditation, allow yourself to sit quietly for a couple of minutes—this helps you to again take in your surroundings before embarking on your next activity.

MEDITATION ON THE KUNDALINI SHAKTI AND THE SVAYAMBU LINGAM

This meditation subtly works on the feminine and masculine energies within you.

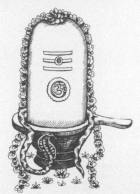

Decide on a definite time for your meditation—minimum time ten minutes. Assume meditation posture. With concentrated but relaxed attention, focus on an image of Kundalini Shakti, the serpent, radiating like the sun, coiled around Shiva, the Svayambu Lingam, radiating like the moon. You can use an external pictorial reference or allow the image to emerge within you.

The Muladhara chakra is also connected to **Ganesha,** the elephant-headed God, son of the Divine Mother Shakti, consort of Shiva. An important deity, revered in Hinduism as the remover of all obstacles, his protection is invoked at the beginning of all ceremonies and endeavors.

MEDITATION ON GANESHA

The effectiveness of this meditation depends on acceptance of Ganesha as a powerful protector and remover of obstacles. It also involves acceptance of his physical form, which is symbolic of his inner power, generosity, and compassion.

The four arms of Ganesha represent aspects of his service in removing obstacles. In one hand, he holds a hatchet indicating the severance of bondage to the passions and the erroneous identification of the self with the body. Another hand is held in a mudra of fearlessness. The third hand holds a lasso, representing the imprisonment of worldly attachments and the reining in of desires; and in the fourth he holds a "sweet delicacy"—chickpea flour made into a tasty aromatic ball, symbolizing sattva, the purest form of consciousness. It is these qualities that the aspirant attends to in contemplating Ganesha, as well as being open to the energies that are subtly working on his or her being.

For this practice, follow the preliminaries for the meditations on the other deities. Allow ten to fifteen minutes.

With relaxed yet concentrated attention, focus on an image of Ganesha. Be mindful of the implements he holds and their symbolic meanings.

Note the effects of your meditation in your Workbook Journal.

WORKBOOK EXERCISES

1. Continue to write down your experiences and the effects of all the practices of this chakra in your Workbook Journal. After three to four weeks of adhering to these practices, note any particular changes you have noticed. Note also your ongoing reflections in response to the questions raised in this chapter. In addition, write down your responses to the following.

2. The Muladhara chakra controls the sense of smell. In some people this sense is relatively undeveloped, in others it is highly developed, and in others somewhere in between. On a scale of one to ten, how would you rate your general awareness of smell? Write down six of your favorite smells and a brief comment on why you like these smells. Then write down six smells that you particularly dislike and a brief comment on why you dislike them.

3. The smell of our bodies changes at different times according to what we apply to our body, what we eat, if and when we fast, or when we are unwell. Are you familiar with your own body odor? If not, start noticing the smell of your body at different times of the day during a one-week period and write down what you notice. Repeat this during the different seasons of the year and write down your observations. Enlist the help of a family member or friend and write down what you notice about their smells.

4. Have the same person arrange eight to ten objects—including some food items—in numerical order, without you seeing, then blindfold you and lead you to smell each item in turn without you touching or tasting any of them. Say out loud to your friend what you think the item is and check your score at the finish. Note also your responses to the exercise. Reverse roles with your family member/friend. Share your responses.

CHAPTER FIVE

THE SVADISTHANA CHAKRA

Learn about the second chakra and its characteristics. Where is the second chakra located? How do you awaken this chakra through meditation on sound, mantra, yantra, and its deities?

Svadisthana is the second chakra, or lotus. The name is derived from *sva* (self) and *adhisthana* (abode or dwelling place) and means "abode of the self" or "one's own abode."

Location Genital area.

Color Orange or silver, light blue or transparent (like water).

Tattwa/Element Water—the life-giving essence of physical life. Water constitutes three-quarters of the weight of the human body—in blood, saliva, mucus, lymph glands, urine, and other fluids. It also covers three-quarters of the earth's surface.

Lotus Deep red with six petals. The color of this lotus indicates the energies of creativity, desire, and sexuality. It also represents imagination, impulses, and ideas that stimulate the mind. The petals signify six levels of being or mental qualities: infatuation, delusion, disdain, suspicion, pitilessness, and destructive tendencies.

Letters on the Lotus Petals Bam, bham, mam, yam, ram, lam.

Seed Sound/Bija Mantra Vam.

Vehicle of the Seed Sound Makara, an alligator-type creature, the vehicle for Varuna, the Vedic lord of the waters, God of the ocean, rivers, and lakes. Makara's wide-open mouth swallows up everything indiscriminately, signifying a gullible or credulous quality as well as devouring appetites. Makara likes to hunt, is tricky, quietly watches intended prey waiting for the right moment to pounce, and likes to play in the waters. These characteristics are indicators of second-chakra consciousness—it enjoys the thrill of the chase, likes to pretend or play-act, can be devious, and is consumed by fantasies, desires, and appetites for sex, food, and pleasure.

Associated Female Deity Shakti Rakini.

Associated Male Deity Vishnu.

Associated Sense Taste.

Sense Organ Tongue.

Associated Plexus and Glands Hypogastrium, sacral plexus, adrenal glands.

Associated Parts of the Body Genitals—"the work organ," prostrate, uterus, large intestine, bowel, bladder, pelvis, lower vertebrae, hip area.

Ruling Planet Mercury.

Associated Astrological Signs and Planets in Western Astrology Gemini and Mercury; Cancer and Moon; Libra and Venus; Scorpio and Pluto.

CHARACTERISTICS

Muladhara chakra energies are concerned with the primal instincts, the group-mind consciousness of our cultural group or tribe, and survival, self-preservation, and security, but Svadisthana chakra energies reach beyond this. They are concerned with exploring relationships beyond the family and cultural group, with exerting greater independence and with exploring the creative and sexual drives. Sexual excitement, the pleasure principle, entertainment, "creature comforts," imagination, and fantasy are all related to second-chakra energies. The personality expands to exploring identity, imagining other ways of living, envisioning wider choices, establishing friendships, and expending effort to impress others—particularly to attract a desired sexual partner. Idealism, romantic love, and heroic feats hold particular appeal. Desire, which is fundamentally creative desire, matures in the desire for love. In the second chakra, the desire for the highest enjoyment of life, which is in actuality the supreme bliss of Self-realization, takes the form of a yearning for intimate sexual pleasure that leads to a committed relationship.

The Svadisthana chakra's connection with procreation of life and its preservation, relates to changes in family relationships and familial responsibilities. The young person starts to assert her or his identity, which tests the norms and boundaries of those relationships. At this time, the family, while depended upon, can begin to seem restrictive, as can society. This can manifest in rebelling against rules, regulations, external discipline, and societal norms—the "rebel without a cause" or the "rebel looking for a cause" exemplifies this attitude, which stems from a natural impulse to exert greater control over his or her life-choices and destiny. Normally, children between eight and fourteen years of age act from second-chakra concerns.

What may be normal attitudes and behavior for adolescents are unhealthy when carried too far into adulthood. A person whose energies are concentrated in this chakra will often be hedonistic, jealous, moody, changeable, and preoccupied with sexual desires and fantasies or excessively concerned with or addicted to the pleasurable sensations of food, sex, alcohol or other drugs, and material comforts. Conversely, a person whose energies in this chakra are diminished or blocked will usually be sexually inhibited and immature—

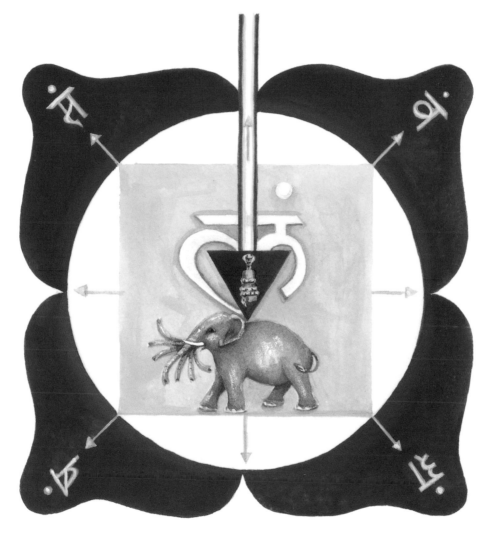

Figure 1: Muladhara, the first chakra

Figure 2: Svadisthana, the second chakra

Figure 3: Manipura, the third chakra

Figure 4: Anahata, the fourth chakra

Figure 5: Visuddha, the fifth chakra

Figure 6: Ajna, the sixth chakra

Figure 7: Sahasrara, the seventh chakra

Figure 8: The seven chakras

perhaps sexually dysfunctional, emotionally distant, and lacking the ability to form satisfying close relationships. This diminished energy will impoverish sensuality and produce an inability to enjoy the simple, natural pleasures of life.

Other symptoms of diminished second-chakra energy are timidity, guilt, resentment, and hypersensitivity. A state of meaninglessness and purposeless can also manifest in a second-chakra person. An aspect of the second chakra is establishing boundaries; however, when a person resents discipline and perceives the world as unfriendly and social norms (other than those in truly oppressive regimes) as obstacles and oppressive restrictions, a negative attitude can develop.

The energetic imbalances in this chakra can occur in puberty, when hormonal changes and awakening sexual energies may cause confusion and uncertainty. Many people experience a lack of bodily contact, of comforting touch, tenderness, and affection in the early years, and this often leads to inhibition or inappropriate expressions of natural sexual energy. This can manifest in either suppressed drives, which intermittently erupt in some way, or in an excessive preoccupation with sexuality and sexual fantasies—in some cases, with sexual addiction. In these instances, the natural creative potential of sexuality remains undeveloped. Sexual expression will be limited and unrefined and pushed either into the foreground or the background of life. Attitudes to the opposite sex or the desired sexual partner will tend to be ambivalent and uncertain, causing underlying tension in a relationship. This may give rise to feelings of discontent or yearning for a satisfying relationship, without the realization that the cause of the dissatisfaction lies within the self and not with another person.

ENERGY BLOCKAGES

Unbalanced or blocked Svadisthana chakra energies can manifest as single or multiple disorders that indicate either a deficiency or excess of energy in this center.

PHYSICAL DISORDERS

The second chakra influences the genital organs, kidneys, lower vertebrae, pelvis, large intestine, appendix, bladder, and hip area. Physical disorders may therefore include chronic lower-back pain, sciatica, arthritis, pelvic problems, intestinal disorders, urinary-tract problems, skin problems, impotency, gynecological problems, reproductive disorders, and ovarian or prostate cancer.

PSYCHOLOGICAL DISORDERS

These can include:
- addictions
- sexual dysfunction
- sexual inhibitions, perversions, or impotency
- exhibitionism
- superficiality
- inauthentic/false personality
- jealousy, envy, resentment
- aimlessness, hedonism, selfishness
- deception, living in a fantasy world
- shallow relationships, poor relationship choices
- shame about the body and/or sexuality
- reckless behavior that continues into adulthood
- restlessness, irresponsibility, prolonged emotional or sexual immaturity
- problems managing money, control issues
- pessimism, anxiety, suicidal tendencies, and destructiveness

TRANSCENDING THE SVADISTHANA CHAKRA

In order to transcend this chakra, we must endeavor to exert moderation in our appetites, have regular physical exercise, develop self-discipline, seek suitable avenues of creative expression, be sexually and financially responsible, ethical in our behavior, and honest in our relationship with ourselves and "others," and seek balance in our lives.

Balancing or unblocking the Svadisthana chakra energies can manifest as resilience and self-discipline and the ability to:

- assume responsibility for our lives
- initiate, make decisions, and take risks
- stand on our own both physically and financially
- reject what is not in our own and others' best interests—and establish another life direction if necessary
- protect and defend ourselves physically and emotionally
- assert healthy boundaries
- exert control over and direct our sexual and creative drives and desires
- keep in touch with our emotions
- increase our powers of intuition

Balancing the energies can also enhance our generosity, creativity, spontaneity, enjoyment of life, cooperation, respect for the rights and dignity of others, capacity for empathy, and our willingness to share, be intimate, and enjoy mutually empowering relationships.

 WORKBOOK EXERCISES

As with the Muladhara chakra, read carefully through this section and list any physical or psychological disorders that you can relate to—giving yourself scale ratings as before—and for each one list three possible strategies for inner and outer change. Also refer to the Workbook Exercises at the end of this chapter.

AWAKENING THE SVADISTHANA CHAKRA

Meditations for awakening and balancing the energies of this chakra are assisted by the presence of its related element, water. Meditations in the presence of water are said to strengthen the immune system and increase vitality.

As discussed earlier, powerful karmic energies, both active and inactive, are housed in the Muladhara and Svadisthana chakras and must be taken into account when awakening these chakras. When the Kundalini Shakti is awakened and begins to ascend, both inactive karma (housed largely in the Svadisthana chakra) and active karma are unleashed. The superconscious mind housed in the Ajna chakra is said to be completely aware of the functioning of the unconscious mind in the Svadisthana chakra and therefore able to control the unleashed karmic energies. If you have not already done so, go now to Chapter Nine and follow the practice instructions for awakening, clearing, and harmonizing the Ajna chakra. When this chakra is awakened and cleansed, work on the Muladhara chakra and then come back to this chakra.

YOGA PRACTICE FOR AWAKENING THE SVADISTHANA CHAKRA

This practice, when performed with a still body and mind in a deeply meditative attitude, is called *vajroli* in yoga. It is usually done in conjunction with a technique called **khechari mudra**, which needs to be learned from an experienced yoga teacher. These practices can also be done independently, as both incorporate aspects to stimulate the Svadisthana chakra. There are two parts to the practice.

AWAKENING SVADISTHANA: PART ONE

Place a small bowl of water nearby or sit in meditation near a watercourse. Sit in sukha asana, easy posture, on a meditation stool or chair. For meditation posture, see page 44.

As with all meditations and visualizations, begin by doing a few minutes of simple relaxation breathing (page 48) or simple pranayama practice (page 49) for five rounds.

Keeping your body relaxed, press your palms against your knees, lift the shoulders slightly upward and forward, and keep the elbows locked straight. Bend your head down and press your chin firmly against the top of the sternum. This is *jalandhara banda* (chin lock). Close your eyes, keep your body as still as possible, and breathe naturally.

Now concentrate directly on the Svadisthana chakra. Focus on the particular area of your body associated with this chakra and allow your awareness to locate the chakra point in the energy field of your body. While maintaining concentration, slowly contract and relax the muscles in the surrounding area. Begin by contracting and relaxing the chakra point and slowly expand this area to include the genitals. Ensure that the area of the Muladhara chakra remains relaxed. It usually takes a little time to isolate the different muscle groups, but this can be resolved by ongoing practice. The muscular contractions and relaxations need to be done slowly and deliberately, with full awareness.

AWAKENING SVADISTHANA: PART TWO

After practicing in the above pose for a few minutes, resume your meditation posture and continue the muscular contractions and relaxations. After practicing for whatever time you have allocated, sit in a simple meditation posture and chant **OM** (**A-U-M**) three times.

Note the effects of your experience in your Workbook Journal. This will help you to monitor the changes occurring in your system.

MEDITATION FOR ENERGIZING THE SVADISTHANA CHAKRA

Place a small bowl of water nearby where you can see it without strain as you meditate, or use an oil burner with a few added drops of ylang ylang, sandalwood, frankincense, or patchouli essential oils. The presence of water can help develop vitality and freedom from disease, enhance your sensitivity, creativity, and attractiveness, and boost intellectual agility. In this meditation, you meditate on the element water itself. As with the yoga practice for awakening the Muladhara chakra, this is a process of meditating on the tip of the nose (see pages 57–58), adding concentration on an aspect of the Svadisthana chakra.

Your focus can be on the water you have placed nearby or on a picture of a water environment such as a lake, ocean, river, or waterfall. This can also be done as a visualization practice—imagine a favorite water environment or create a waterscape scene in your mind's eye. This meditation can also be done sitting in a bath or pool of still water—a wonderful variant to the usual sitting meditation practice. However, make sure the water temperature is such that you can remain warmly comfortable for the duration of your meditation. Also, ensure you are in a draft-free environment and will not be disturbed.

 ENERGIZING SVADISTHANA

This is a process of meditating on the tip of the nose while concentrating on an aspect of the Svadisthana chakra. Place the bowl of water or the picture of water nearby. Align it with your downward gaze around the tip of your nose.

Adopt your meditation posture. Maintain a still and relaxed body, keeping the spine straight and aligned with the neck and head. Do simple relaxation breathing (page 48) or simple pranayama practice (page 49) for a few minutes. Hold, in your awareness, the area of the body associated with the Svadisthana chakra. Keep your downward gaze on the water element aligned with the tip of your nose and open to the energy of the water element. Remain open to each manifestation and what lies within it and what lies within that. Continue to breathe naturally and notice what arises while letting all flow through you.

SOUND

Here is an exercise for intoning the Sanskrit letters **bam, bham, mam, yam, ram, lam** inscribed on the lotus petals. These are pronounced **bang, bhang, ngang, yang, rang, lang.** This practice is similar to the sound meditation mantra practice of intoning the bija mantra **vam** (see page 80).

As with other practices, when beginning this meditation, do it on its own in sitting meditation for four to six weeks. Acclimatize yourself to any one practice before combining it with another practice. Decide on a time for your mantra practice—say, five to ten minutes in the beginning stages. Adopt your meditation asana or sitting position. Do a few minutes of simple relaxation breathing (page 48) or pranayama practice (page 49) for five rounds.

SOUND MEDITATION

Begin to intone **bang, bhang, ngang, yang, rang, lang** out loud, and continue for the duration of the meditation. At the end of your meditation, sit quietly for a few minutes; notice the silence and the energy in and around your body.

Take a few minutes to write down the effects of your meditation in your Workbook Journal.

SOUND MEDITATION—MANTRA

In this meditation you continuously repeat the bija mantra of the tattwa of the Svadisthana chakra—which represents water. Have some water nearby. The mantra is **vam,** pronounced **vang.** This practice is similar to the sound meditation practice of intoning the letters on the petals of the lotus (see page 79).

When beginning this mantra meditation, practice it by itself for a few weeks. When you become familiar with the practice, you can combine sounding the mantra **vang** with a visualization practice on the element water or meditation on the yantra (see page 82). Decide on a time for your mantra practice—say, five to ten minutes in the beginning stages.

SOUND MEDITATION—MANTRA

Focus your attention on the image of the Svadisthana chakra while sounding the mantra. Follow this pattern of practice when sounding the mantra **vam.** Adopt your meditation posture. Do a few minutes of simple relaxation breathing (page 48) or simple pranayama practice (page 49) for five rounds. Produce the sound **vang** by pursing the lips in a circle, then sounding the mantra. Push the sound through the lips and resonate it as if coming through a pipe. Try to sound the mantra in the note D following middle C and see how this feels. If uncomfortable, find your own note and stay with that pitch. Concentrate on the symbolic image of the Svadisthana chakra and intone **vang** out loud continuously for the duration of the meditation. At the end of your meditation, sit quietly for a few minutes; notice the silence and the energy in and around your body.

Take a few minutes to write down the effects of your meditation in your Workbook Journal.

YANTRA

The circle and crescent represent water and the moon respectively. The close connection of water and the moon is seen in the governing influence of the lunar phases on the ebb and flow of ocean tides and on the body's biochemistry. As the Svadisthana chakra is associated with the genitals, it is connected with procreation—sexual attraction, the semen in the testes, vaginal fluids, and the menstrual cycle in women. As well as a symbol for water, the circle also represents protection. The connection between water and moon is linked to the emotions. The fluid motion of water is also symbolic of a changeable nature, flexibility, permeability, and sensuality.

The circle is light blue or pale gray-blue, and the crescent silver or white. The moon and water element are also connected in our breathing cycle in the activation of the Ida Nadi in left-nostril breathing. Ida Nadi is lunar in nature, and the left nostril is connected to the right hemisphere of the brain, which relates to emotional behavior. Because of the influence of the lunar phases on a woman's menstrual cycle, as well as on her body's storage of fluids during menses, along with women's receptive nature (receiving the seed, like the earth), the moon is closely associated with feminine energy. The moon's capacity to reflect the light of the sun is also representative of female and male energies, as well as the ability to reflect the "light of awareness."

YANTRA MEDITATION AND VISUALIZATION

When practicing this meditation, have some water nearby to enhance your meditation. As with the other meditations on the Svadisthana chakra, having the element water nearby increases vitality, creativity, sensitivity, and intellectual power.

When you gaze at the circle, reflect on the properties of water and its symbolic associations—and stay open to the images, insights, and intuitions these reflections may bring to the surface. Like thoughts that arise in meditation, you may notice what arises— but do not get carried away by the changing currents. Simply notice, stay internally detached, and remain singly focused on the object of the meditation. Allow the blue colors of water and the silver-white of the moon to permeate your energy at the Svadisthana chakra area when gazing at the circle and the crescent.

At the beginning of the meditation, you could pose a question related to the element of water when gazing at the circle or one related to the moon when gazing at the crescent. However, this practice is not one of analytical thought but rather one of staying open to whatever arises. For subsequent practice, you may wish to reflect on the qualities of water addressed in the Workbook Exercises (page 83).

Note the effects of your meditation in your Workbook Journal.

Try this meditation at each phase of the lunar cycle and note what arises. Remember that the subtle energies are always working their quiet magic underneath your conscious mind.

WORKBOOK EXERCISES

After noting your experiences of the yantra meditation and visualization in your Workbook Journal, reflect on the following questions and write down your responses.

1. Write down five different qualities you associate with water.
2. Briefly describe ten of your observations/experiences of water in nature.
3. The nature of water is to flow. When it doesn't flow it becomes stagnant and susceptible to impurities. Write down three areas where you feel your life has become stagnant.
4. Write down three things that come to mind after reading this: "Water, shapeless in itself, takes on the shape of its container. This can symbolize its ability to reflect its surroundings and its relationships."
5. Water cleanses, nourishes, and renews. List three aspects of your life that need cleansing, nourishment, and renewal.
6. Water is an essential and precious resource. Rate your responsible use of water on a scale of one to ten. If you feel you can improve this score, write down and adhere to four courses of action you can take to achieve this.
7. Do this exercise quickly—honestly noting your first thoughts, sensations, or feelings. List ten words you associate with the word "emotion." Briefly write down what you make of this list. Periodically come back to the list and extend each association by repeating the exercise.
8. Write down five qualities you associate with the moon.
9. On a scale of one to ten, rate your awareness of the cycles of the moon throughout any given year.
10. For women: List four things that describe your menstrual cycle. Write down four changes you notice at each stage of your cycle. List four ways you are managing the changes that occur during your menstrual cycle.

DEITIES

ASSOCIATED FEMALE DEITY (FORM OF KUNDALINI): SHAKTI RAKINI

Keeper of the door of the Svadisthana chakra, Shakti Rakini represents the feminine aspect of Energy manifest. She has two heads, indicating duality of consciousness (the "I" and "the other," the within and the without), with three red eyes, protruding teeth, and a fierce appearance. Her skin, variously depicted in pink or red shades, represents the bodily fluid of blood—connection to the menstrual cycle and flow, which is connected to the cycles of the moon. She may also be depicted with blue skin, representing the creative aspect of the Goddess. She is said to be ecstatic with drinking ambrosia, the **amrit** or **amrita** (nectar) that flows from the Sahasrara chakra and the Divine Energy it infuses within her. Her furious demeanor is said to be a signifier that uncontrolled desire or uncultivated imagination can be dangerous to the psyche—and can make us deluded or mad. We can become exalted, inspired, and ecstatic from harnessing our desires and tasting the bliss of the Divine or fearsomely deluded or mad from uncontrolled fantasies or desires.

Shakti Rakini has four arms, each with a symbol. A trident/arrow, symbol of the Hindu Trinity, also symbolizes the oneness of body, speech, and mind and their interplay. The stick represents the spine, within which Kundalini Shakti is active. The arrow is from Kama, lord of erotic love. It represents the focus of desire on its object and also one-pointed attention—attention only sustained until the arrow hits its target, like romantic love, which thrives on obstacles, fantasies, and "the chase" rather than real intimacy. She also holds an ax or battle-ax, which represents the battle of everyday life and a tool for cutting through the obstacles and negative characteristics that daily hinder our development. She also holds a lotus, symbolizing guiding thought toward purity of mind and sacredness, recognizing that the true Self within all is eternally pure and remains unpolluted by any experience. A drum in another hand represents nada and mantra and rhythm. The rhythm of the drum also represents heartbeat. The drumbeat marks time and rhythm cycles, gives rise to the impulse to move and to dance, as well as stirring emotions, excitement, and sexual feelings. Steady drumbeat can also induce altered states of consciousness.

MEDITATION ON SHAKTI RAKINI

The best times for this meditation are during the twilight hours of dawn and dusk, when the energy is calm, pure, and clear. Again, have the element water nearby—simply a small bowl of water may be best. The presence of water in this meditation is said to lead to emotional connection with Vishnu, who pervades all forms.

Decide on a time for your meditation. Try to allow at least twenty minutes to begin with—including relaxation breathing time and notation time at the end.

Adopt your meditation posture. Yoga practitioners should adopt siddha asana or siddha yoni asana, ensuring the left heel (or right heel if easier) is tucked in closely to the perineum for men or the labia majora for women. Others should adopt either the easy posture or other sitting position—either on a floor cushion or a chair—without leaning against the back of the chair. Ensure your body is relaxed and comfortable and your spine straight. Breathe naturally. Begin with a few minutes of simple relaxation breathing (page 48), or simple pranayama practice (page 49) for five rounds.

With concentrated but relaxed attention, focus on an image of Shakti Rakini—in her exalted, inspired, and ecstatic state from drinking the amrit, the nectar that flows from the Sahasrara chakra, and the Divine Energy that it infuses within her. Also contemplate the symbolic meanings of the implements she holds (see page 84). Meditation on Shakti Rakini enables her battle-ax to cut through the negative mental qualities of infatuation, delusion, disdain, suspicion, pitilessness, and destructive tendencies.

At the end of your meditation, allow yourself to sit quietly for a few minutes.

Make a simple notation of your meditation experiences in your Workbook Journal. Make notes again when you do this meditation at a later stage. Compare your notes.

ASSOCIATED MALE DEITY: VISHNU

Vishnu, the God of Preservation, is the second aspect of the Hindu Trinity (Brahma, Vishnu, and Shiva). Vishnu symbolizes the intelligence on this level and signifies the masculine aspect of Divine Energy unmanifest. He represents the fundamental aspect of preserving life after Creation.

"Vishnu" derives from *vish* (pervasion). Vishnu pervades all life—every atom, every cell—all of Creation. The universe itself is his preserve, maintained by his great spiritual power. Preservation is helped by prana and energies that combine to assist in the healthy growth of an organism. Vishnu also maintains the delicate balance between the life-creating energies of Brahma and the destructive energies of Shiva. Sometimes he has to incarnate to restore equilibrium between these energies when they have become disturbingly unbalanced (as is the case in our own era).

Vishnu has blue skin and is clothed in yellow-gold. Sometimes he is depicted riding Garuda, a mythic bird like an eagle—the king of the birds. He wears a celestial garland of forest wildflowers from the four seasons, extending down to his knees.

Depicted with four arms, he holds in each hand an implement for maximum enjoyment of life through attainment of the four objects of achievement: *dharma* (principles of right living and natural law), *artha* (wealth), *kama* (the celebration of beauty), and *moksha* (ultimate liberation). He holds a conch shell containing the sound of ocean waves, representing the primordial sound **OM (AUM)**, and mantra (pure sound), carrier of enlightenment or liberation, and this also represents the ability to listen attentively and hear what is being communicated. He also holds a mace or club, an object for subduing or killing: the power to control the egoistic personalities and demolish obstacles. A chakra—golden disk of light—spins on the index finger, symbolizing consciousness, poise, concentration, and balanced movement. It also signifies dharma; its continuous spinning creates the cosmic rhythm, the cycle of time, and the eternal play of consciousness. Vishnu also holds a lotus, the preeminent symbol of the sacred, of purity, of the spiritual goal.

The lotus is an exquisite flower, rich in symbolic meaning. It floats on the surface of water (of the mind), is open to akasha (the sky or space), is still (representing equanimity), and luminous (spiritual radiance), yet is connected to the kanda (bulb—originating point of the major nadis), which is rooted in mud (earth, unconscious potential, transformation of human "mire"). The lotus is the quintessential symbol of beauty and the sheer joy of beauty.

MEDITATION ON VISHNU

The preliminaries are the same as for the meditation on Shakti Rakini.

Begin your meditation practice. Start by simply focusing on a picture of Vishnu, which can evoke a sense of peacefulness—like a calm lake with the moon reflected on the water's surface. When you are familiar with the image, try instead to invoke the presence of Vishnu in your mind's eye. Be aware of the symbolic meaning of Vishnu—the Preserver, he who pervades all forms as well as embodying dharma, the principles of right living. Contemplate his nature as the protagonist of the cosmic drama as well as the play, the *lila* (divine sport) of life. Be aware also of the symbology of the implements he holds (see page 86).

If your attention wanders, gently bring yourself back to the focus of your meditation. At the end of your meditation, allow yourself to sit quietly for a few minutes and notice how you feel. This time will also help you to take in your surroundings once more before moving on to your next activity.

Note your meditation experiences in your Workbook Journal.

OM (AUM) is the source of all sound.

WORKBOOK EXERCISES

In addition to noting in your Workbook Journal the effects of the chakra meditations and other practices, ask yourself the following questions and write down your responses. Don't labor over your answers. If a response is not forthcoming, simply turn the question over to your unconscious mind. If something pops out later, write it down then; also note the context if this seems relevant.

1. Write down six ways that you express your sexuality.
2. List six things that sex means to you. Now order this list, with one being most important.
3. If you are not in a sexual relationship by choice or chance, list five thoughts/feelings you have about this.
4. List five ways that you express affection and five ways that you receive affection.
5. List ten things you find most pleasurable in life.
6. The Svadisthana chakra controls the sense of taste. List eight of your favorite tastes. Refer also to the Muladhara chakra questions on smell and extend these to the sense of taste.
7. Do you have any addictions? If so, list them and briefly note five things that you perceive hold you to that addiction/s. What are you doing to overcome these addictions?
8. On a scale of one to ten, rate the state of your relationships with: your "significant other" (if applicable), family members, closest friends, coworkers (can include community members), and neighbors.
9. List five things that you associate with creativity and five ways you express your creativity. If you do not express yourself creatively, list five things that restrain you.
10. On a scale of one to ten, rate how responsible you see yourself to be.
11. Write down three things that express your relationship to money.
12. On a scale of one to ten, rate how honest you perceive yourself to be.
13. Write down five things that you associate with independence, dependence, and interdependence.
14. Write down, without any self-censure, six ways you balance your everyday needs and wants with ethical principles. This is not about judgment but understanding.

CHAPTER SIX

THE MANIPURA CHAKRA

Learn about the third chakra and its characteristics. Where is the third chakra located?
How do you awaken this chakra through meditations on sound, mantra, yantra, and
its deities?

Manipura is the third chakra, or lotus. The name comes from the Sanskrit *mani* (gem or jewel), *pura* (dwelling place or city), and *nabhi* (navel). The Manipura chakra is called the place of gems, the jewel of the navel, or jeweled city. This chakra is often called the solar-plexus chakra. It is our personal power center.

Location Within the Sushuma Nadi, on the inner side of the spinal column, behind the navel region.

Tattwa/Element Fire. Fire signifies purification. It consumes all. Also relates to "digestive fire."

Color Red-gold or yellow-gold.

Lotus The color of heavy rain clouds, which signifies not seeing clearly. The lotus is also blue like the inner flame of a fire. The qualities associated with the ten petals are spiritual ignorance, treachery, jealousy, shame, aversion, delusion, thirst, inertia, sadness, and fear. The qualities of this lower center are negative and still connected to the levels of animal consciousness. Meditating on these qualities, with the open intention of releasing their negative hold, makes it possible to transform them. For example, treachery can be transformed into loyalty, shame into honor, sadness into joy, inertia into motivation, and so on.

An important quality transformed at this level is fear. It is said that where there is fear, there is power. To move beyond fear is to feel grounded, powerful, and fearless. This unleashes healing and strengthening energy from our navel area that flows throughout our system. Our overall health and sense of well-being can be seriously eroded by toxic emotional environments, so it is vital that we address fear in all aspects of our lives. When we work toward transforming our personal fears, the beneficial effects impact on our entire being.

Letters on the Lotus Petals Dam, dham, nam, tam, tham, dam, dham, nam, pam, pham.

Seed Sound/Bija Mantra Ram.

Vehicle of the Seed Sound The ram, vehicle of Agni, Vedic lord of fire. The ram is associated with the fire element and the planet Mars. It signifies the nature of a third-chakra person. An active animal, renowned for its wiry strength, stamina, and combative disposition, the ram fights its opponents head on and does not easily surrender or retreat. This signifies an ability to meet challenges directly and to endure. The ram can also have a headstrong and stubborn nature.

Associated Female Deity Lakini (Laksmi).

Associated Male Deity Rudra (Old Shiva).

Associated Sense Sight.

Sense Organ The eyes.

Associated Plexus and Glands Solar plexus, epigastrium, adrenal glands.

Associated Parts of the Body Stomach, upper intestines, pancreas, liver, gall bladder, the middle spine—located behind the solar plexus—and the muscles. The "work organs" are the legs and feet.

Ruling Planet Sun.

Associated Astrological Signs and Planets in Western Astrology: Leo and Sun; Aries and Mars; Sagittarius and Jupiter; Virgo and Mercury.

CHARACTERISTICS

The Manipura chakra energies govern puberty, from ages fourteen to twenty-one. The energies in this chakra help to further the processes of forming an identity, the "I-consciousness" or ego, and the personality differentiated from the family, the cultural group, and the inherited tendencies—our karmic inheritance. The Manipura chakra is also the gravitational point of the body.

Of particular significance are the powers that connect in the Manipura chakra. Here, the three major nadis, Ida, Pingala, and Sushumna, originate in the kanda (see Chapter Two). This forms an opening through which our consciousness can ascend to the Sahasrara chakra. The navel is a very important area. All mammal embryos are connected to the mother by the umbilical cord and are nourished through it. Similarly, all the pranas flow together in the Manipura chakra and distribute from there the subtle pranas of the food nourishment we ingest.

Known as the personal power center, the Manipura chakra, like the Muladhara and Svadisthana chakras, still relates primarily to physical and external forms of power—albeit with a different focus. In the first chakra, power was connected to the cultural group, tribe, and employer, and in the second chakra, to relationships with others. In the Manipura chakra, power relates to our sense of personal power and our relationships with the outside world. The energies of a third-chakra person are centered on the personal self. This manifests in asserting identity, pursuing ambitions, seeking recognition, and improving position or status in life.

A DRIVE TO SATISFY DESIRES

Vision and form are strong aspects in this chakra. You may become interested in social trends, status symbols, and fashion. All such preoccupations can lead to disregarding others in the drive to satisfy desires and goals. A sense of achievement can be gained from attaining goals, but pride and arrogance may develop from experiencing the ability to control and manipulate others and life circumstances to suit ourselves.

INFLUENCE OF THE FIRE ELEMENT

This chakra's association with the fire element can manifest as anger, impatience, and intolerance, particularly when expectations aren't met. Fiery outbursts, simmering looks, disapproving or resentful body language, and emotional distance can be used to manipulate or intimidate others into submission. The fire element can also lend a passionate dimension to the personality, which can be quite compelling. If the natural outpouring of energies in this chakra is blocked, however, a person may become inhibited, lacking in confidence and direction.

The designated color of the ruling planet, yellow-gold or red-gold, connotes warmth and vitality. Like the sun, yellow is also related to the mind and the intellect. Intellectual power plays an important part in the orientations, behavioral expression, and relationships of a third-chakra person.

When the Manipura chakra is not purified, its fire can burn us in our desire and hunger for worldly pleasure. However, when the Kundalini Shakti is awakened and this center is being purified, the fire becomes a fire of purification, which burns up all of our negative qualities. The sacred texts tell us that we can offer up our negative qualities to the Divine fire that resides within us—we can do so in our meditations and visualizations.

ENERGY BLOCKAGES

Unbalanced or blocked Manipura chakra energies can manifest as single or multiple disorders that indicate either a deficiency or excess of energy in this center.

PHYSICAL DISORDERS

The third chakra influences the stomach, upper intestines, pancreas, liver, gall bladder, middle spine (located behind the solar plexus), and the muscles. Physical disorders possible include stomach or digestive disorders such as indigestion, ulcers, gastritis, and poor assimilation of nutrients; diabetes; hypoglycemia; liver problems; muscle stiffness or cramps; and nervous tension.

PSYCHOLOGICAL DISORDERS

Problems may be experienced with self-worth, responsibility, hypersensitivity, and overreactivity to perceived criticism, a need for external validation, and fear of rejection. This can result in low self-worth, lack of confidence, inhibitions, insecurity, excessive concern with physical appearance, vanity, narcissism, and depression. If not addressed, these issues can lead to physical illnesses in the areas associated with the third chakra—though all illness affects the whole system of a person.

Other energy disorders are greed, rigid conformity, a resentful attitude toward authority, a judgmental attitude, egotism, selfishness, self-absorption, workaholism, perfectionism, assertion of rights ahead of responsibilities and/or failing to meet responsibilities, and a restless dissatisfaction with life.

To transcend this chakra, we need to develop an honest understanding of ourselves and appreciate and accept our strengths and weaknesses. As we work through this process, we gain self-acceptance, self-worth, and self-respect. When we confront our fears, again and again, and move through them, we develop confidence and the courage to take risks. We become more willing to take the initiative and meet the responsibilities of our actions. We also develop the ability to cooperate with others, share, and serve—without seeking recompense or approval.

BALANCING THE ENERGIES

When the Manipura chakra energies are balanced or unblocked, this can manifest as self-respect, respect for others, self-acceptance, self-responsibility, confidence, self-discipline, strength of character, and ethical behavior. There can be improvement in motivation, awareness of the effect of our actions upon others, and the ability to take risks, better negotiate life's challenges and crises, and initiate action. When empowered, we become willing to engage openly with the world and enjoy life more as we allow ourselves to be more charitable and willing to do things for others without the need for personal gain or recognition. Greater generosity of spirit emerges, generating emotional warmth and relaxation of being.

WORKBOOK EXERCISES

As with the Muladhara and Svadisthana chakras, read carefully through this section and note, again without censoring or judging yourself, any physical and psychological energy disorders that may apply to you. After you have done this, write down your responses to the following questions in your Workbook Journal.

1. The Manipura chakra is the center of personal power so this is an opportune time to look at issues related to power in your life and relationships.
   • List ten things you associate with the word "power."
   • On a scale of one to ten, rate how confident you feel. Now rate how confident you feel in different aspects of your life, for example, in your relationships and in your work.
   • List six things that give you a sense of self-worth.
   • Do you give away your power? If so, list to whom and in what situations. Briefly note three things in each case that you perceive is behind this tendency.
   • On a scale of one to ten, rate how motivated you see yourself.
   • List six things you associate with the word "strength"—both inner and outer.
   • On a scale of one to ten, rate your willingness to take initiatives and to take risks.
   • Write your own definition of the word "courage."
2. It is said that where there is fear, there is power. Note three things that this statement evokes in you.
3. If you have a fear of rejection, write down four things that you associate with rejection.
4. On a scale of one to ten, rate how honest you see yourself.
5. Do you experience feelings of jealousy and envy? If so, write down three reactions you have to such feelings.
6. On a scale of one to ten, rate how critical you are of yourself and of others.
7. Think of a time in the past when things have not gone as you wanted. Write down how you reacted to this. Have you reacted to similar situations in the same way?
8. Write down five aspirations you currently have. Now write down three strategies you have for attaining each of these aspirations.

AWAKENING THE MANIPURA CHAKRA

Meditations for awakening and balancing the energies of the Manipura chakra are assisted by the presence of fire, this chakra's related element. This can strengthen the body's natural immune system and aid longevity. Place a lit candle or oil lamp in a stable, draft-free position nearby.

Sit in the meditation posture of your choice. Place hands on knees, palms facing downward. Begin with a few minutes of simple relaxation breathing (page 48), or simple pranayama practice (page 49) for five rounds.

Close your eyes. Focus on the tip of your nose or the space between the eyebrows. Maintain this focus, keeping your eyes gently closed and the surrounding eye muscles relaxed. Inhale deeply, and imagine the prana in the breath being absorbed through the throat and flowing down to the navel. Hold your breath.

Contract the rectal and perineal muscles and draw them upward. Imagine apana—the pranic energy that dwells in the area between the navel and rectum—flowing up from the Muladhara chakra to the navel.

While holding your breath, concentrate on the navel and visualize the unification of prana and apana there. Hold this contraction for as long as you can comfortably hold the breath. When you begin to feel pressure to release the breath, release the contraction, then slowly exhale. Repeat this cycle for ten minutes to begin with.

It takes a bit of practice to be able to isolate and contract the muscles of the perineum and rectum and strengthen those muscles so you can hold the contraction firmly. This will happen naturally with repeated practice. As you become more familiar with the practice, gradually increase the time, in increments of five minutes, to twenty or thirty minutes.

SOUND

As with the first and second chakra sound meditations, the letters on the lotus petals are intoned: **dam, dham, nam, tam, tham, dam, dham, nam, pam, pham.** These letters are pronounced **dang, dhang, rlang, tang, thang, dang, dhang, nang, pang, phang.** As with the other meditations, the practice is enhanced by the presence of the related element—fire in this case. This meditation is similar to the sound practice of intoning the bija mantra **ram.**

SOUND MEDITATION

As with the earlier sound practices, when beginning this meditation, do it on its own in sitting meditation, and practice for four to six weeks. Decide on a time for your sound meditation practice—say, five to ten minutes at first.

Adopt your meditation asana or sitting position. Do a few minutes of simple relaxation breathing (page 48) or simple pranayama practice (page 49) for five rounds.

Intone **dang, dhang, rlang, tang, thang, dang, dhang, nang, pang, phang** out loud continuously for the duration of the meditation. At the end of your meditation, sit quietly for a few minutes; notice the silence and the energy in and around your body.

Take a few minutes to note the effects of your meditation in your Workbook Journal.

SOUND MEDITATION—MANTRA

In this meditation we continuously repeat the bija mantra of the tattwa of the Manipura chakra, which represents fire. As with the other meditations, the practice is enhanced by the presence of the chakra's element. The mantra is **ram,** pronounced **rang.** This practice is similar to the sound meditation practice of intoning the letters on the petals of the lotus (see page 97).

SOUND MEDITATION—MANTRA

As with all new practices, do this on its own in sitting meditation and practice it for four to six weeks. Decide on a time for your mantra practice—say, five to ten minutes at first. Adopt your meditation asana or posture. Do a few minutes of simple relaxation breathing (page 48) or simple pranayama practice (page 49) for five rounds.

To produce the sound, first purse your lips with the mouth slightly open. Then press the tongue against the palate and sound **rang.** Experiment with sounding the mantra in different pitches, including E above middle C, and hold this pitch if comfortable—if not, find a more comfortable pitch and hold for the duration of the practice.

Take a deep breath, and while concentrating on the image of the Manipura chakra, intone **rang** out loud continuously for the duration of the meditation.

At the end of your meditation, sit quietly for a few minutes. As with the previous sound meditations, notice the ensuing silence and the energy in and around your body.

Take a few minutes to note the effects of your meditation in your Workbook Journal.

YANTRA

The shape is a bright red inverted triangle located in the center of the lotus. There is an "auspicious" swastika on each of its three sides. The swastika is an ancient symbol and has many interpretations, depending on the particular belief system with which it is associated. In Hinduism the swastika is a symbol of Agni, the Vedic lord of fire; the Hindu Trinity; the cycle of creation–preservation–destruction; and Vishnu and other deities. It is also associated with solar and generative symbols. In this instance the swastika is said to represent eternity.

The inverted triangle suggests the downward movement of energy. It forms an obstruction to the upward energetic movement of Kundalini Shakti until it is pierced by transcending material concerns and attachments and being able, through sustained practice, to maintain one-pointed concentration in meditation. In these ways the path is cleared for Kundalini Shakti's ascension to the higher chakras of awareness. The simple geometric form of the triangle, with three equal sides, suggests balance, the trinity, and the containment and directing of powerful energy. It also resonates the number three—with all of its associations, such as the three *gunas* (qualities), the *tripura* (three worlds), the three aspects of consciousness, the three modes of experience, and the three *granthis* (knots), which have to be pierced by Kundalini Shakti in her upward journey of spiritual awakening. Meditation and visualization on this yantra help to harness the power of the Manipura chakra.

YANTRA MEDITATION AND VISUALIZATION

Meditation or visualization of the bright red yantra triangle helps in our spiritual evolution. Practice this meditation in the presence of fire. Simply place a lit candle in a stable, draft-free position nearby. As with other meditations on the Manipura chakra, the presence of the element of fire boosts the body's natural immunity, aids longevity, and releases particular and unusual powers of authority, management, and leadership.

YANTRA MEDITATION AND VISUALIZATION

Decide on a time for the meditation. Place an image of the yantra where it can be seen easily. Adopt your meditation posture. Begin with a body scan, and notice those areas that feel tense. Practice simple relaxation breathing (page 48) for a few minutes. Breathe into those areas that feel tense, and release the tension on the out breath.

The meditation can begin by focusing on either the swastika or the inverted triangle. If you begin with the swastika, follow this by focusing on the inverted triangle. Reverse this order if you begin by focusing on the inverted triangle.

As this yantra represents the element of fire, reflect on the significance of fire. There is the fire that consumes and transforms matter from one state to another. There are the heat- and light-producing qualities of fire. There is emotional fire—the heat of passions, of anger, of sexuality. There are the purificatory aspects of fire, which burn away the dross and cleanse and clear systems of debris in the physical, subtle, and spiritual realms. There is the radiant fire of the sun—with its life-giving qualities to the physical world and its association with the celestial realms and the sacred inner flame of Spirit. Fire can blaze out of control or its power can be harnessed and directed. Reflect on these qualities of fire and how they manifest in your life.

As you face honestly the negative aspects of fire in your life, imagine them being consumed in the flames one by one and then being purified. Imagine yourself walking through the fire of purification. Notice what arises.

Create the intention to work on those areas in your life that need purification and to act on your directives. This may involve some painful decisions and processes if major change is flagged, for it is necessary to transcend the negative energies of the first three chakras in order to ascend successfully to the higher chakras. If you practice daily contemplation and meditation, this will strengthen your inner resolve and fan the flame of Spirit within, which will nourish and support your journey.

WORKBOOK EXERCISES

When you have finished the yantra meditation and visualization practice, allow a few minutes to write down in your Workbook Journal what has arisen for you and any intuitive directives you may have been given.

In addition to this practice, you can also meditate on fire itself. Sit in front of a blazing fire or visualize sitting by a fire or campfire. You can also vary this by imagining a scene of brightly burning flames in your mind's eye. Follow the same instructions and reflections as on page 100.

Write your responses to the following questions in your Workbook Journal.

1. List six things that you associate with the word "fire."
2. Fire symbolizes purification. List five areas in your life that need purifying.
3. List five emotions that you associate with fire.
4. List eight things you associate with the word "passion."
5. On a scale of one to ten, rate how passionate you feel you are. Now rate how passionate you feel in different aspects of your life, for example, in your relationships and in your work.
6. Fire burns away the dross and clutter of life. Write down four aspects of your life that need clearing of clutter in each of these areas—physically, mentally, emotionally, and in relationships. For your physical list, note three possible strategies for clearing the space you seek. With your mental and emotional lists, ritually burn them and sincerely offer their contents to the Divine power for transformation. For your relationship list, write down three undertakings and adhere to them—despite possible lapses from time to time. Also respond to the Workbook Exercises at the end of this chapter.

DEITIES

ASSOCIATED FEMALE DEITY (FORM OF KUNDALINI): LAKINI (LAKSMI)

Lakini signifies the feminine aspect of Energy manifest. She is the Divinity, the Shakti—the Power or Energy—of the Manipura chakra. She is also the Goddess of abundance. Striking in appearance, her skin is either "dark" or a peach-orange-pink color. She has three faces with three eyes in each face. The face is the seat of all five senses. They show us that the range of vision in the Manipura chakra encompasses the physical, the astral, and celestial planes; the faces also signify ego, mind, and intellect. The third eye (the Ajna chakra area) signifies increased power of clairvoyance—inner sight—that is potentially available.

Lakini has four arms, each holding a symbol. A thunderbolt signifies the power in nature to ignite what it strikes, and electrical energy that continuously emanates. A fire weapon, or fire pot, indicates the energy of fire, the fire of purification, and the physical heat said to radiate from within her body. A hand gesture grants fearlessness and blessings. She holds an arrow or uses another mudra. The arrow signifies aspiration and the goal to be free, independent, accomplished, and authoritative. The mudra here is in a gesture of granting boons and dispelling fears.

MEDITATION ON SHAKTI LAKINI

Again, the best times for meditations on the deities are the twilight hours of dawn and dusk, when the energy is clear and calm. Have the element of fire nearby to enhance the meditation and assist in developing beneficial qualities of body–mind–spirit. Meditation on the deities of the Manipura chakra begins with Lakini and then Rudra (Old Shiva). Lakini is said to assist in guiding an aspirant to meditation on the calm and pure manifestation of Rudra.

Decide on a specific time for your meditation. Place a picture of Lakini where it can be seen without strain or practice internal concentration on the qualities of Lakini at the Manipura chakra. Assume your meditation posture. Begin the practice with a few minutes of simple relaxation breathing (page 48) or five rounds of simple pranayama practice (page 49).

Meditate on Lakini as the keeper of the door to the Manipura chakra, which sparkles like a precious jewel. Be mindful of Lakini as a dispeller of fears and provider of abundance and also of the symbolic meanings of the implements she holds (see page 102).

At the end of your meditation, sit quietly for a few minutes; notice the energies in and around your body.

Note the effects of your meditation in your Workbook Journal.

ASSOCIATED MALE DEITY: RUDRA (OLD SHIVA)

Rudra is the destroyer aspect of Shiva. He signifies the masculine aspect of Energy unmanifest, and the intelligence on this level. He dissolves the world at the end of its cycle so a new cycle of Creation may begin. Like the consuming fire, Rudra dissolves everything within himself. All existence returns to him.

Rudra's skin is red, but appears to be old and white—his body is smeared with purificatory ashes, which show the necessity of purifying our passions and emotions to transform their energies and ascend to the higher chakras and higher levels of awareness. Ashes also signify death. The personal ego needs to die to realize the spiritual Self, and it is important to detach from physical and material concerns and concentrate more on our inner being—our feeling and spiritual Self. There is also the inevitable death of the physical body—ashes to ashes—and the return of the Spirit to its eternal Home.

Rudra is also depicted with a lustrous white beard and dressed in a tiger skin. He sits on a tiger skin, which, like his own skin, is smeared with ashes. The tiger represents the mind. Rudra is depicted with either two or four arms. He holds a trident, symbol of Shiva and the Hindu Trinity, and also holds a drum—representing the heartbeat, keeper of time, the pulse of life, and also fatality. When depicted with four hands, the third hand holds a particular rosary for mantra japa (mantra repetition). The fourth hand is held in a symbolic gesture for granting boons or dispelling fears.

Sometimes Vishnu in his preservation aspect is called the Deva of the Manipura Chakra, representing power over the imagination and strong emotions and the definitively human consciousness that has its beginning in this chakra.

MEDITATION ON RUDRA (OLD SHIVA)

The best times for the meditation on Rudra (Old Shiva) are during dawn or dusk. Again have the element fire nearby—a lighted candle or oil burner.

Rudra is said to free an aspirant from worldly attachments—which appear as **Brahma Granthi** (the "knot" of Brahma) in the Manipura chakra. This is one of three knots, or obstructions, that have to be loosened in order for someone to be truly spiritually liberated. The three knots represent three aspects of consciousness. The "knot" of Brahma represents feeling and the mind, as well as attachments to the phenomenal world and the illusory world of names and forms.

Decide on a time for your meditation. Try to allow at least twenty minutes at the beginning—including relaxation breathing time and notation time at the end.

Adopt your meditation posture. Ensure your body is relaxed and comfortable and your spine straight.

Begin with a few minutes of simple relaxation breathing (page 48) or simple pranayama practice (page 49) for five rounds, then breathe naturally.

Begin your meditation practice. Start by simply focusing on a picture of Rudra or on the qualities of Rudra as the holder of all spiritual knowledge. As with the other deities, focusing on Rudra evokes a sense of peacefulness. When you are familiar with Rudra, instead of focusing on a picture representation, try to invoke the presence of Rudra in your mind's eye. Be aware of the symbolic meaning of Rudra, and the symbology of the implements he holds (see page 104). If your attention wanders, gently bring yourself back to the focus of your meditation.

At the end of your meditation, allow yourself to sit quietly for a few minutes. This will help you to take in your surroundings again before moving on to your next activity.

Note the effects of the meditation in your Workbook Journal.

The dancing Energy of the spiritual heart, the cosmic dance of life, is symbolized
by Shiva in his well-known form as the Nataraja—the Lord of the Dance.

WORKBOOK EXERCISES

1. Continue to write down the experiences of your practices in your Workbook Journal.
2. The Manipura chakra controls the sense of sight.
   - List ten words you associate with the word "sight."
   - Note what is most important to you about being able to see.
   - Write a paragraph on how you imagine it would be not to be able to see.
   - Refer to the questions in Muladhara chakra on smell and Svadisthana chakra on taste and extend these to sight.
3. List the most important characteristic that gives you a sense of purpose. Then list four other factors that also assist your aspirations.
4. List the strongest factor that you feel may hold you back in life. Are there other factors? If so, list them.
5. Do you suspect that self-sabotage is at work in certain areas of your life? If so, list those areas and the ways your self-sabotage is operating.
6. On a scale of one to ten, rate how responsible you see yourself to be.
7. On a scale of one to ten, rate your decisiveness.
   - Note four instances in the past month or so when you were decisive. What were the outcomes? List the factors—whether seemingly positive or negative.
   - Note four instances in the past month or so when you were indecisive. What were the outcomes? If the situations are still in process, note that down—list factors involved.
8. Do you have a tendency to procrastinate? If so, write down three areas where this is particularly manifested. Also write down three possible reasons why you procrastinate in each area.
9. On a scale of one to ten, rate how selfish/self-centered you feel you really are. List four traits or areas where this quality is apparent.
10. Write down six words that you associate with the word "change."
11. List eight of what you see as your strengths and eight of what you see are your weaknesses. When you read through this list, note what arises within you.

CHAPTER SEVEN

THE ANAHATA CHAKRA

Learn about the fourth, or Heart, chakra and its characteristics. Where is the fourth chakra located? How do you awaken this chakra through meditations on sound, mantra, yantra, and its deities?

Anahata is the fourth chakra, or lotus. This Sanskrit name means "unstruck" and is derived from anahata-sabda, the unstruck sound. Sound is usually produced by striking objects together. This emanates sound waves or vibrations, which are detected through auditory mechanisms. However, the unstruck sound that is the mystical anahata-sabda is heard by yogis and sages without the striking together of objects. This is the **Sabda Brahman**—the Absolute in the form of sound. The Anahata chakra is also called the Heart chakra and is revered in many spiritual traditions as a center of love, devotion, equilibrium, compassion, and transformation. The Anahata chakra is the seat of **hamsah** (the individual soul) and the seat of balance.

Location In the center of the spine at the center of the chest or the heart region of the spinal column.

Tattwa/Element Air.

Color Green or smoke (as in the color of smoke rising from a flame).

Lotus Vermilion, or deep red, with twelve petals splayed outward from the circle containing the yantra. The petals represent the qualities of anxiety, possessiveness, egotism, lustfulness, duplicity, conceit, indecision, incompetence, regret, hope, endeavor, and discrimination. Whereas the qualities in the three lower chakras are all negative, those of the Anahata chakra are a mixture of negative and positive.

Letters on the Lotus Petals Kam, kham, gam, gham, nam, cam, cham, jam, jham, nam, tam, tham.

Seed Sound/Bija Mantra Yam.

Vehicle of the Seed Sound Black antelope or musk deer, vehicle of Vayu, Vedic lord of the wind. The deer or black antelope is a symbol of the heart. The antelope is similar to the deer—both symbolize movement, speed, and gentle grace. They are fleet of foot, with a dancing gait and a restless nature. This represents an impressionable nature and also the fleeting nature of spiritual experiences difficult to grasp by the novice heart. The deer is a shy creature and very sensitive to sound, reacting to the faintest whisper of threat, real or imagined. It has big, beautiful, velvety eyes that reflect guilelessness—symbolic of innocence and purity. Black is often used to signify depth and mystery, which are also qualities associated with the heart.

It is said that the deer dies to pure sound. This suggests that the ego self, the "I-consciousness," dies when it recognizes the pure unstruck sound of the Absolute in the Heart. The "i" is then absorbed into the "I"—the goal of the spiritual path.

Associated Female Deity Shakti Kakini.

Associated Male Deity Isha—a form of Shiva.

Associated Sense Touch.

Sense Organ Skin.

Associated Plexus and Glands Cardiac plexus, thymus gland.

Associated Parts of the Body Heart, circulatory systems, lungs, ribs, diaphragm, breasts, shoulders, arms, and hands—the "work organ."

Ruling Planet Venus.

Associated Astrological Signs and Planets in Western Astrology Libra and Venus; Taurus and Venus; Leo and Sun; Saturn.

CHARACTERISTICS

The Anahata chakra energies govern the period from twenty-one to twenty-eight years of age. These energies focus on our emotional terrain, creating awareness of emotional responses; the currents of thoughts, attitudes, and actions; how we attend (or don't attend) to our emotional needs; and our motivations, inspirations, goals, and greater purpose in life. It is in the Anahata chakra that we begin to learn about the greater power of love and the pathways of the heart.

A fourth-chakra person has risen above the domination and preoccupations of the first three chakras: the drive for survival and security of the Muladhara chakra, the sexual and sensual desires and addictions of the Svadisthana chakra, and the egotistic thirst for making a mark in the world through ambition, fame, authority, "power over," social status, material acquisition, and so on that are the focus of Manipura chakra energies. The lower chakras involve our relationships with the external world. In the Anahata chakra we turn within and begin to learn about the inner world of our experiences. It is in the Anahata chakra that we begin the process of self-knowledge. This involves challenges, trials, healing, and transformation.

Commitment, steadfastness, trust, and self-confidence are strong motivating and sustaining forces as we strive to attain balance in the various dimensions of our lives. Following a spiritual path makes the attainment of our goals easier and helps to rein in impulses to chase after pipe dreams or grasp at straws out of fear, reactivity, unclear purpose, or restlessness—like the deer or the antelope. But the deer is also graceful and gentle, with beautiful eyes. The eyes are often said to be "the windows of the soul," and the open childlike gaze of the deer is symbolic of the at-once innocent and wise, pure, and soul-soothing qualities of an evolved fourth-chakra person.

OPENING TO LOVE

Although a natural spiritual inclination occurs with the opening of the Anahata chakra, as it is an opening to love, this may not necessarily manifest in the adoption of a formal spiritual direction if we are not already following a spiritual path. As love is the Good, it may inspire us to be good in our lives and relationships—to be kind, friendly, empathetic, compassionate, selflessly giving, accepting, and so on. Such an attitude brings peace and grace into the manifest world, which is a movement of Spirit, even though not specifically defined as such, and the effects are felt nonetheless. Truth and the Good are not in the definitions, but in the felt experience.

The challenge of this chakra is to open to love, to heal past wounds to the heart, and to resolve the reactionary behavior based on unhealed wounds so that we may come to a place of acceptance—of ourselves and the way things are. This process leads naturally to forgiveness of others and of ourselves. We are then enabled to move through the Anahata chakra to the higher chakras and to live openly in the present, unencumbered by past emotional detritus. In this way we learn how to act out of empathy, love, and compassion and recognize that the most powerful and liberating energy we have is love. It is by going through the trials of the heart, going within and learning its lessons, that we begin to discover what is really meant by "To Thine Own Self be True."

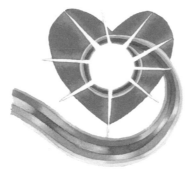

ENERGY BLOCKAGES

Unbalanced or blocked Anahata chakra energies can manifest as single or multiple disorders that indicate either a deficiency or excess of energy in this center.

PHYSICAL DISORDERS

This chakra influences the heart, the circulatory systems, lungs, ribs, diaphragm, breasts, shoulders, arms, and hands, so disorders of energy tend to manifest in these areas.

PSYCHOLOGICAL DISORDERS

These include fears of being alone, commitment, rejection, betrayal, and emotional weakness. Unhealed wounds related to love in our early relationships can later give rise to possessiveness, jealousy, anger, codependency, an inability to follow the directives of the heart, and the inability to forgive others as well as ourselves. Also possible are excessive emotional neediness; being judgmental, overly critical, and demanding; moodiness; passive aggression; emotional coldness and manipulation; overattachment to people and objects; and the need for constant external reassurance. This in turn can lead to alienation, grief, bitterness, hatred, revenge, paranoia, an inability to express love, and a questioning of the very existence of love.

In order to transcend this chakra we must endeavor to clear and cleanse our hearts, minds, and bodies of past emotional wounds arising from relationships and injuries to trust. Only then can we truly open our hearts to the healing power of love—and freely give to all.

BALANCING THE ENERGIES

When the Anahata chakra energies are balanced or unblocked, this can manifest as emotional warmth, friendliness, kindness, empathy, patience, serenity, harmonious relationships with the natural world and with others, respect, compassion, unconditional love—for oneself and others—openness, generosity, willingness to share, devotion, trust, hope, faith, inspiration, balance, acceptance, commitment, dedication, the ability to let go and go with the flow, spontaneity, joy, and the ability to forgive the self and others.

WORKBOOK EXERCISES

As with the Muladhara Chakra, read carefully through this section and note any physical or psychological energy disorders that may particularly apply to you. After you have read through this section, write down your responses to the following questions in your Workbook Journal.

1. Do you suffer from any heart problems, circulatory disorders, asthma, lung disorders/diseases, and/or high blood pressure? If so, note any disorders, and for each one, list your thoughts about the causes of these disorders and your current approaches to treatment and its effects to date.

2. Do you have unhealed wounds related to family members, close friends, and/or other significant relationships? If so, write down what they are and list four factors that gave rise to your feelings of emotional pain and four factors that sustain this pain. List four things you feel are needed to begin the healing process for these wounds.

3. Do you make decisions based primarily on mental processes or on emotional responses —or a mixture of both? Whichever the case, write down five factors involved in your decision-making process. If a mixture of head and heart is involved, note how you perceive that and the particular life areas where one or the other dominates.

4. On a scale of one to ten, rate the degree of external validation you need from others to feel a sense of personal value.

5. What is more important to you—work/career success or your relationships? List five reasons why this is the case.

6. Write down your four greatest fears in relationships.

The Anahata chakra is the midway point of balance between earth energies and the higher, more subtle energies. The color visualization on page 116 is an exercise to balance those energies—in conjunction with the other practices for this chakra.

AWAKENING THE ANAHATA CHAKRA

This practice requires breathing with full awareness on the in breath. Being in the presence of the element of air—in the atmosphere, in your breathing, and in visualizations—will enhance all meditations and visualizations for the Anahata chakra. The presence of the element air will help develop personal magnetism, intellectual power, heightened perception, inner beauty, and attractiveness.

Adopt a comfortable, supportive posture and stay relaxed. However, where other meditations require you to keep the body–mind as still as possible, with this practice you can adjust your position to maintain comfort if needed. The usual preliminaries apply. Adopt your preferred meditation posture and gently close your eyes. Practice a few minutes of simple relaxation breathing (page 48). Breathe into any tense areas of your body and relax them on the out breath or do five rounds of simple pranayama practice (page 49).

AWAKENING ANAHATA: PART ONE

With your eyes gently closed, concentrate on the throat. Inhale with full awareness on the incoming breath. Feel the breath in your nostrils and its passage going down deep into your chest cavity. Stay in the space of this awareness rather than attending to the outgoing breath.

Now direct your awareness to the space just above your diaphragm and inhale. Notice this space being filled by the incoming breath and also the filling process itself.

Continue to breathe normally—don't force the breath in any way—and in time you will begin to feel the space around your heart.

Once awareness of the heart-space has developed and become established, you will feel it expanding and contracting in rhythm with your breath. If you do not feel this at first, simply focus on feeling the breath filling the space, as above. Then try the following steps.

AWAKENING ANAHATA: PART TWO

Once you are established in the practice and if the awareness of the heart-space, along with its expansion and contraction, is steadily maintained, an image will appear in the heart-space. Do not try to visualize anything; just allow the image to arise naturally in its own time. This may or may not happen in the early stages of this practice. The important thing is to let the image appear by itself when ready.

At the end of your meditation, open your eyes and notice how you feel.

MEDITATION TO OPEN THE HEART CHAKRA

This is a simple and soothing breathing meditation on the heart that can be done anytime you need nurturing, release, or tranquility. It is enhanced by the presence of the element air.

Decide on a time for your meditation—from ten to twenty minutes. Ensure you are in a quiet place to avoid interruptions. Adopt your preferred meditation posture. Close your eyes and focus on the tip of your nose. Feel the breath coming in and out of your nostrils.

Now bring your awareness to the space in the middle of your chest. Breathe into that space and feel it expand naturally. Continue to breathe normally and allow your awareness to go deeper into that space.

An image may arise. Simply observe it without any mental effort to hold onto it. Maintain your awareness of the space and the breathing as images come and go. If emotion arises, notice what it is and what it is connected to, but let it be—allow it to flow through without any mental directives or judgment. Allow all to come and go in the heart-space of awareness and continue to breathe normally.

At the close of your meditation, bring your attention back to the tip of your nose for a few minutes. Now open your eyes, notice how you feel, and take in your surroundings.

COLOR VISUALIZATION TO HARMONIZE THE ENERGIES OF THE ANAHATA CHAKRA

This visualization meditation can be done sitting, standing, or lying down in *shava asana* (corpse posture)—on your back, with legs slightly apart, and arms out diagonally to the side with palms facing up.

The best times for this meditation are first thing in the morning or last thing at night. If sitting, adopt your preferred meditation posture. Close your eyes and breathe normally. Be aware of the element air in the breath. Practice a few minutes of simple relaxation breathing (page 48) to relax the body and quiet the mind.

With your eyes gently closed, feel the presence of your Heart chakra in the middle of your chest. Now visualize the color black deep in the earth.

On inhaling, breathe the color black up from deep within the earth into the feet, up the legs, up through the center of the body, to above the Sahasrara/Crown chakra. When you have reached the peak of the in breath, visualize the color gold, and with the exhalation, take the gold color down through the crown of your head (area of the Sahasrara chakra), down through the center of the body, down the legs, feet, and into the earth. Repeat this breathing pattern for ten breaths. This is one cycle.

Bring your awareness again to the Heart chakra area and continue to breathe normally for a moment or two. Now repeat the color visualization practice cycle. Practice this for five rounds.

Complete the practice by again bringing your awareness back to the Heart chakra and breathing normally. Open your eyes and notice how you feel.

Note your experiences in your Workbook Journal.

Cautionary note: If you start feeling dizzy, resume normal breathing with your focus on the area of your Heart chakra and then resume the practice.

SOUND

Here is an exercise for intoning the Sanskrit letters **kam, kham, gam, gham, nam, cam, cham, jam, jham, am, tam, tham** inscribed on the lotus petals. These are pronounced **kang, khang, gang, ghang, uang, cang, chang, jang, jhang, uang, tang, thang.**

This practice is similar to the sound meditation mantra practice of intoning the bija mantra **yam** (see page 118). Be aware of the element air—around you, in the breath, and in the air inside the mouth.

SOUND MEDITATION

When beginning this meditation, do it on its own in sitting meditation and practice it for four to six weeks. Decide on a time for your meditation practice—say, five to ten minutes to begin. Adopt your meditation posture or sitting position. Do a few minutes of simple relaxation breathing (page 48) or simple pranayama practice (page 49) for five rounds.

Intone **kang, khang, gang, ghang, uang, cang, chang, jang, jhang, uang, tang, thang** out loud continuously for the duration of the meditation. At the end of your meditation, sit quietly for a few minutes; notice the silence and the energy in and around your body.

Take a few minutes to note the effects of your meditation in your Workbook Journal.

SOUND MEDITATION—MANTRA

In this meditation you continuously repeat the bija mantra of the tattwa of the Anahata chakra. The mantra is **yam,** pronounced **yang.**

This practice is similar to the sound meditation practice of intoning the letters on the petals of the lotus (see page 117). Again, be aware of the element air—around you, in the breath, and in the air inside the mouth.

As with previous chakras, when beginning this meditation practice, initially do it by itself in sitting meditation. Decide on a time for your mantra practice—say five to ten minutes to begin. Adopt your meditation posture. Do a few minutes of simple relaxation breathing (page 48) or simple pranayama practice (page 49) for five rounds.

SOUND MEDITATION—MANTRA

Bring your awareness to your Heart center (and the yantra when combining it with visualization). The sound **yang** is produced with the tongue first touching the palate and then resting in the air inside the mouth. Again experiment with different pitches, including F above middle C, and see which pitch feels most comfortable for you in this chakra. Stay with this pitch.

Now begin to intone **yang** continuously out loud for the duration of the meditation. At the end of your meditation, sit quietly for a few minutes; notice the silence and the energy in and around your body and how you feel.

Take a few minutes to note the effects of your meditation in your Workbook Journal.

YANTRA

Within the lotus circle is a six-pointed star, symbolizing the air element, with two interlocked, intersecting triangles—one pointing up and one pointing down. The upward-pointing triangle symbolizes the higher, or spiritual, nature and the aspirant's journey to that higher power. The downward-pointing triangle signifies the lower nature of humans and the animal–human consciousness and is linked to earth energies.

The star signifies the balanced union of opposites: the upward-pointing triangle represents the solar masculine principle and the downward-pointing triangle the lunar feminine principle. It also symbolizes the mediating and balancing of energy in the Anahata chakra between the three chakras above it and the three chakras below it. The six points of the star indicate that the element air can move in all six directions—upward, downward, and in the four directions.

The four directions on the body also symbolize a cross, with the Heart chakra in the middle, balancing the left side of the body—yin, female—with the right side of the body—yang, male. When inspired by love, compassion, and the impulse to share, the movement of energy can be upward to Spirit and downward to Earth and harmonize and integrate these energies. In the Anahata chakra, we open to the power of love.

THE ANANDA KANDA

Inside the yantra is another lotus, luminous red with eight petals, located to the right of the physical heart and below the Anahata chakra. In the center of this lotus, a heart is depicted representing the spiritual heart known as **Ananda Kanda,** or the "Space of Bliss." It is also known as the **Hrit Pundarik** (Heart lotus). The innately pure and physically untainted Ananda Kanda is a seat of the Divine Self and is prescribed in many meditative traditions as a place of inner worship. When a meditation practice instructs focusing attention on the heart, it is to the Ananda Kanda that an aspirant is being directed. It is said that this center can only be reached when the Sushumna Nadi is activated.

YANTRA MEDITATION AND VISUALIZATION

When practicing this meditation, be aware of the element air in your surroundings and in the air flowing in and out of your nostrils. As with the other meditations on the Anahata chakra, being in the presence of the element air is said to cultivate personal magnetism, inner beauty, attractiveness, intellectual power, and heightened perception. It can also lead to the development of creative writing and poetic abilities.

When you gaze at the yantra, contemplate its shape and structure (see page 119). Reflect on the properties of air and its symbolic associations—and stay open to the insights that may arise.

The two triangles of the star represent the harmonious intertwining of spiritual and earthly energies. They also symbolize the mediating and balancing of energy in the Anahata chakra. In the body, the spiritual energies enter through the Sahasrara/Crown chakra, the earth energies enter through the feet, and both energies meet in the Anahata chakra. Reflect on this and how these energies are within your own body.

Reflect on the feminine and masculine energies in your system. What does this mean to you, and how do you experience this in your body and awareness?

At the beginning of the meditation, you could pose a question related to the element air when gazing at the star. You could also pose a question related to the balancing of earthly and spiritual energies and the feminine and masculine energies when gazing at the interlocked triangles. However, as with previous meditations and visualizations, the practice is not one of analytical thought, but one of staying open to whatever arises.

Finish the practice with a few minutes of relaxed breathing. Focus on the air coming in and out of your nostrils.

Make a note of your meditation experience in your Workbook Journal.

WORKBOOK EXERCISES

The tattwa or element of the Anahata chakra is air. Air cannot be seen but it can be felt—but not grasped and held. Air indicates both stillness and movement and is associated with lightness. Air contains prana and is essential for life.

Write down your responses to the following reflections and questions in your Workbook Journal.

1. List six words you associate with the word "air." As before, do this quickly and write down the first word that comes to mind and then move on to the next.
2. Write down ten effects of air.
3. Write down six sounds that you associate with the movement of air.
4. Right at this moment and without changing anything, notice your breathing. Is it shallow, deep, or in-between? Rate your breathing on a scale of one to ten. Do this exercise a dozen times over the next week—whenever it comes to mind—and note each observation. At the end of the week, review your results and write down what you discover.
5. Write down six words you associate with the word "wind."
6. When the phrase "there is something in the air" is used with regard to a situation, what does this elicit in you? List three things.
7. Sometimes people are described as having a certain "air" about them. List three things that come to mind in response to this statement.
8. Become more conscious of air in your daily life. After a month or so, note what you have noticed.

DEITIES

ASSOCIATED FEMALE DEITY (FORM OF KUNDALINI): SHAKTI KAKINI

Keeper of the door of the Anahata chakra, Kakini represents the feminine aspect of Energy manifest—symbolizing self-generating and self-emanating energy. Like air, she is all-pervasive and gives energy to the entire body through the vibrations generated by *bhakti* (devotion). Described as rose-pink or golden yellow with shining eyes, she is luminous in appearance, adorned with a dazzling array of golden ornaments. She is associated with the bodily substance of fat.

Kakini has three eyes, like Isha, and four arms holding implements for attaining balance. These objects vary in different depictions, but convey the same underlying messages. She generally holds a noose and a skull, with her two remaining hands in mudras of granting boons and dispelling fears. The noose represents the necessity of harnessing passions, desires, worldly influences, and expectations—including spiritual expectations. The skull symbolizes the need to die to the egotistic self of misidentification, vanity, and ignorance, and to become pure mind or empty mind. She may also hold a sword, representing severing obstacles to the upward flow of energy, and a shield, symbolizing protection from worldly influences.

Kakini is also often depicted with four faces, each said to be as lustrous and beautiful as the moon. Like the Shakti divinities in previous chakras, she is depicted in a happy and exalted mood from drinking the nectar that flows from the Soma chakra. The Soma chakra is within Sahasrara chakra and is of utmost importance. It is here that Kundalini Shakti in the form of Kameshvari is united in eternal bliss with Lord Shiva in the form of Kameshvara.

Kakini is free of the wrathful aspects of the Devis of the lower chakras. She is beneficent, joyful, and said to be auspicious. She is the goddess who inspires the creation of love poetry, mystical and devotional poetry, visionary art, and music. Art inspired by Kakini is cosmic in nature, elevates the consciousness, bringing peace and harmony to the person who is the conduit of its creation and to those who witness its manifestations with an open heart and mind.

MEDITATION ON SHAKTI KAKINI

As with the other meditations, the best times for meditations on Shakti Kakini and Isha Shiva are during the twilight hours of dawn and dusk. Again, be aware of the presence of the element air to enhance the meditation and help develop beneficial qualities of body–mind–spirit. Shakti Kakini is said to be graceful, joyful, auspicious, and able to bestow **siddhis** (superpowers). Meditation on the deities of the Anahata chakra begins with Shakti Kakini and continues with Isha Shiva.

Decide on a definite time for your meditation—try to allow at least twenty minutes in the beginning. Include relaxation breathing time and notation time at the end. Place a picture of Kakini where it can be seen without strain or practice internal concentration on the qualities of Kakini (see page 122) in the Heart chakra.

Assume your meditation posture. Begin the practice with a few minutes of simple relaxation breathing (page 48) or five rounds of simple pranayama practice (page 49). Be aware of the air flowing in and out of your nostrils.

Meditate on Kakini as the keeper of the door to the Anahata chakra, which shines like a precious jewel in the center of the spine. This is the radiant center of love, devotion, and transformation.

Focus on Kakini as a "moon-faced" Goddess, handmaiden of the Divine Mother, whose Energy flows from her four heads into the four dimensions of the individual self: the physical self, the sensual self, the rational self, and the emotional self. Be mindful of Kakini as the Goddess inspiring the higher creative and visionary arts and as a protector and benefactress. Also reflect on the symbolic meanings of the implements she holds (see page 122). Note your meditation experiences in your Workbook Journal.

ASSOCIATED MALE DEITY: ISHA—A FORM OF SHIVA

Shiva, as the deity Isha, is overlord of the first three chakras. He represents the masculine aspect of Energy unmanifest. He is frequently depicted with three eyes and two arms. The third eye is the all-seeing "Eye of Wisdom," the fully awakened Ajna chakra situated behind the space between the two eyebrows. Isha often holds the *Trimurti*, a trident—symbol of the Hindu Trinity; and a drum in the left hand. Isha is Shiva in his ever-youthful aspect, described as "the beautiful One," with cool blue skin and the "soft radiance of ten million moons." His hair is matted by the purifying stream of Self-knowledge flowing as the holy river Ganges through his shining locks. This is the knowledge of "I Am That"—the Divine Self—bestowing perpetual happiness, beneficence, equanimity, and peace.

KALPATARU, THE CELESTIAL WISHING TREE

Within the Ananda Kanda (see page 119) is the celestial wishing tree, the Kalpataru, which is the Tree of Life. The Kalpataru grants all that a seeker asks, leading her or him to liberation. At the base of the tree is an ornamental altar or throne adorned with precious jewels. This is the seat of the Divine Self. It is here that we meditate on our Divinity within and the inner flame of unconditional love and bliss.

MEDITATION ON ISHA SHIVA

Once more, be aware of the presence of the element air to enhance the meditation and assist in developing beneficial qualities. Isha Shiva is said to represent detachment from the world—to symbolize that the evolved fourth-chakra person is free of attachments to the material world, worldly pleasures, and all attributions of praise and blame. Meditate upon these qualities.

Decide on a time for your meditation. Try to allow at least twenty minutes. Include relaxation breathing time and notation time at the end.

Adopt meditation posture sukha asana, siddha asana, or siddha yoni asana for yoga practitioners, and sukha asana (easy posture) or other sitting position—either on a floor cushion or a chair—for others. Ensure your body is relaxed and comfortable and your spine straight. Breathe naturally. Begin with a few minutes of simple relaxation breathing (page 48) or simple pranayama practice (page 49) for five rounds. Be aware of the air flowing in and out of your nostrils. Begin your meditation practice.

Start by simply focusing on a picture of Isha Shiva or on his qualities: he is detached from worldly concerns and pleasures, in harmony with the internal and external worlds, and has balanced energy in all six directions. Focusing on all deities evokes a sense of peacefulness; in this case, detachment can also be evoked.

Be aware of the symbolic meaning of the implements he holds (see page 124). If your attention wanders, gently bring yourself back to the focus of your meditation. When you are familiar with Isha Shiva, instead of focusing on a picture representation, try to invoke his presence in your mind's eye. Or continue to focus on the qualities symbolized by Isha Shiva.

At the end of your meditation, allow yourself to sit quietly for few minutes. Note your meditation experiences in your Workbook Journal.

SHIVA AND THE BANA LINGAM

Shiva also resides at the center of the lotus circle in a red downward-pointing triangle. The triangle represents Shakti, the feminine principle, whose gentle body has been described as being like "ten million flashes of lightning." The lingam represents Shiva, the masculine principle, and in this chakra is known as **Bana Lingam.** It is radiant gold, as the sun, and represents Shiva in the aspect of eternal benefactor, as the Sabda Brahman—the Absolute in the form of sound, and in the sacred syllable **AUM** or **OM.** This is the second Shiva Lingam in the chakra system—first is the Svayambu Lingam and the Kundalini Shakti in the Muladhara chakra, representing masculine and feminine principles. Bana Lingam is said to represent our inner guide who, via the heartbeat, alerts us to correct observance of the dharma of the spiritual path. This is also the site of the **Vishnu Granthi,** the "knot" of the heart, second of the three knots that have to be untied on the path of liberation.

The center of the heart lotus is also the site of a shimmering flame of light, a site of contemplation where we receive abundance from the visible and the invisible realms. This steady flame, unperturbed by wind (worldly activities), represents **hamsah.** The two syllables of hamsah represent Shiva and Shakti. *Ham* is Shiva—the still point, the experiencing subject, the in breath. *Sah* is Shakti, primordial nature, Creation or emanation, the out breath. Hamsah is the union of these eternal polarities and also the Sanskrit word for "swan," often used as a symbol for the soul in Hinduism.

Kundalini Shakti appears as a beautiful Devi for the first time in the Anahata chakra. She sits independently in lotus posture in the center of an upward-pointing triangle and is described as youthful, luminous, self-contained, cool, centered within herself, and serene. She has transcended representation as the destructive serpentine force in the Muladhara chakra and is now a personification of devotion sitting in yogic meditation on her Lord Shiva, the Absolute. She has two forms. One is as an embodiment of *anahata nada,* the universally present cosmic sound, which begins in the Heart lotus as the seed sound **OM,** or **AUM,** and then manifests in sound formations that comprise mantras and speech. She also remains in subtle form, after the dissolution of all sound within her, in a state of consciousness embodying elevated spiritual knowledge.

WORKBOOK EXERCISES

As the Anahata chakra is the center of love, compassion, and balance, reflect on these qualities in all aspects of your life and relationships. After having reviewed the section on Characteristics in this chapter and answered the questions raised, reflect on the following and write your responses in your Workbook Journal.

1. Write down ten things you associate with the word "love." As before, do this exercise quickly.
2. On a scale of one to ten, honestly rate both your openness to receiving love and to giving love.
3. Do you see love as something that comes from outside or inside? Write a paragraph on why you perceive love the way you do.
4. Write down six different types or expressions of love.
5. Write down six qualities you associate with true friendship. Now write down how you know when a friendship is true.
6. Write down six qualities you associate with compassion.
7. Write down six things in life that inspire you.
8. List six qualities you associate with "devotion."
9. Are you able to forgive others and yourself for perceived transgressions? If so, note how you do this. If not, why not—list your reasons and what has to happen for you to be able to allow forgiveness.

A particular expression of the Anahata chakra is the sense of touch. Note your responses to the following:

1. List six words you associate with the word "touch."
2. Do you like or dislike being touched? In each case, write down six reasons why.
3. Write down six ways you express and receive affection.
4. Often people say they have been "touched" or "moved" by someone or something. Drawing from your own experience, write a brief paragraph on what this means.
5. What comes to mind when you read the following quote:
   "Love is the mother and we are her children." (Rumi)

CHAPTER EIGHT

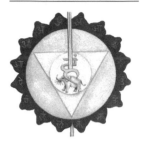

THE VISUDDHA CHAKRA

Learn about the fifth chakra and its characteristics. Where is the fifth chakra located?
How do you awaken this chakra through meditations on
sound, mantra, yantra, and its deities.

Visuddha (or **Visuddhi**) is the fifth chakra, or lotus. The Sanskrit name means "pure" or "pure wheel," from the Sanskrit *vish* (poison) and *shuddi* (pure). Purification and pure knowledge are key aspects of the Visuddha chakra. It is said to be the "gateway of the Great Liberation."

The Visuddha chakra is closely connected to the Bindu-Visarga, a psychic center between the Ajna chakra and the Sahasrara chakra that produces nectar, which the body is not yet able to assimilate as it is burned up by the element fire in the Manipura chakra area. This center is also called the Bindu chakra or Chandra chakra (moon center).

Location The throat; neck region—the part of the spinal column in the neck area.

Tattwa/Element Akasha—space or the void, also called ether.

Color Smoky purple or indigo.

Lotus Sixteen petals around the circle and crescent. The petals are described as smoky purple, lavender, or indigo. There are sixteen qualities associated with the petals, not psychological but predominately connected to musical sound—seven subtle tones (which do not correspond in order with the musical scale) and certain bija mantras used to invoke divinities in the body. The sounds belong to the deities who govern the petals and, when invoked, give energy to the qualities. It is said that in the eighth petal there is poison and in the sixteenth there is nectar; these represent the destructive and constructive forces of the world.

Letters on the Lotus Petals a—a—i—i—u—u—r—r—l—l—e—ai—o—au—am—ah. (These are written here without their Sanskrit accents; also written as am, am, im, im, um, um, rim, rim, lrim, lrim, em, aim, om, aum, am (the in breath—Shiva), and ah (the out breath—Shakti).

Seed Sound/Bija Mantra Ham.

Vehicle of the Seed Sound A snow-white elephant, vehicle of Ambara, the deity connected with the bija mantra and the element akasha/space/ether. The elephant is a living teacher through embodying and symbolizing such qualities as endurance, strength, patience, keen memory, humility, and living in harmony with nature. It also symbolizes the will subdued through surrender. It has large ears and a steady gait, which, in this chakra, represent an attentive attunement to sound and innate rhythm. The elephant's trunk symbolizes pure sound, and its white color spiritual development and purity.

Associated Female Deity Shakti Sakini.

Associated Male Deity Sadashiva.

Associated Sense Hearing.

Sense Organ Ears.

Associated Plexus and Glands Carotid plexus; laryngeal plexus; thyroid gland.

Associated Parts of the Body Neck vertebrae, throat, jaw, organs of hearing, parathyroid, hypothalamus, trachea, bronchial tubes, esophagus, skin, teeth, voice. The mouth and vocal cords are the "work organs."

Ruling Planet Jupiter.

Associated Astrological Signs and Planets in Western Astrology Jupiter and Sagittarius; Gemini and Mercury; Mars; Taurus and Venus; Aquarius and Uranus.

CHARACTERISTICS

The energies of the Visuddha chakra strongly influence people from twenty-eight to thirty-five years of age. The search for deeper meaning in life—that is, the seeking of true knowledge and the need to transcend the impositions of cultural conditioning and the limitations of negative personality aspects—motivates fifth-chakra people. These motivations, when sustained by sincere intent, commitment, and honest self-appraisal, generally lead to spiritual awareness. This process also involves understanding the power of choice in our lives, as there are many emotional and mental struggles involved in the decisions we make and the directions we take, as well as in the consequences involved in these decisions. It is a continuation of the learning: "To Thine Own Self Be True."

The purification of the self and spiritual awakening arise in this chakra. However, the full awakening of the Visuddha chakra and the movement upward to the higher chakras can only really occur when all residual impurities of the lower chakras have been cleansed and purified. As this includes transcending worldly concerns and attachments and the experience of true spiritual knowledge, it usually only occurs for sages, yogis, and authentic spiritual teachers. Spontaneous spiritual awakenings without arduous spiritual practice—even that of Self-realization—do occur, but this phenomenon is said to arise from work done in previous lifetimes.

An interest in religious teachings, scriptures, and ancient wisdom commonly arises in this chakra. However, when knowledge is acquired intellectually but not grounded in disciplined spiritual practice and experience, the ego usually claims such knowledge as its own. This can lead to egocentricity and arrogance and other negative characteristics in a person, and this is evidence of unresolved aspects of the lower chakras. When such negativities are overcome, the person becomes spiritually inspired, and this in turn inspires others.

An important aspect of this chakra is learning to trust. On a personal level, this requires discrimination—in terms of knowing whom and what to trust and learning to trust inner guidance. Courage is also needed in not allowing ourselves to be swayed by external circumstances when we come to trust in ourselves and our inner guidance. This is trust in its deepest sense, which is the surrendering of the personal will and the demands of the ego to the guidance of Divine will. This leads to cocreating with the Divine, as the personal will is in complete union with that of the higher Self.

The Visuddha chakra is also the center of sound, of communication. This involves learning to speak the truth always, to speak clearly, and to use words wisely—which again requires discrimination as well as patience. It also means learning when to speak, when to be silent, and how to speak according to the greater requirements of a situation. An evolved fifth-chakra person understands the true power of vibration, sound, and the word. In the Visuddha chakra, thoughts, feelings, and words become clear.

ENERGY BLOCKAGES

Unbalanced or blocked Visuddha chakra energies can manifest as single or multiple disorders that indicate either a deficiency or excess of energy in this center.

PHYSICAL DISORDERS

This chakra influences the neck vertebrae, throat, jaw, organs of hearing, parathyroid, hypothalamus, trachea, bronchial tubes, esophagus, skin, teeth, voice, mouth, and vocal cords. Some physical problems that can occur include: ear, nose, and throat disorders such as throat infections and sore throats; neck pain, stiffness, and spasm; pain in the back of the head and around the jaw; clenching and grinding of teeth; and speech problems. Also, various skin problems, thyroid disorders, some digestive disorders, and weight problems may occur.

PSYCHOLOGICAL DISORDERS

These include fear of:

- losing control, being out of control in regard to money, power, substances, sex, and another's emotional sway
- having little or no personal authority, having no choice in our lives
- surrendering our personal will to the Divine will

Fears can lead to being shy, timid, unreliable, inconsistent, cunning, devious, manipulative, indirectly and creatively deceitful, shut down emotionally, withdrawn into the mind, arrogant, dogmatic, blunt, self-righteous, judgmental, anxious about sex, and either excessively verbal or frustrated at perceived inadequate communication.

In order to transcend this chakra, we must endeavor to move beyond fear, doubt, and negativity. Fear in this chakra arises from lack of trust in the Divine will and can only be dispelled through surrender and faith. Doubt arises through insecurity about knowledge or the misuse of knowledge. Again, trust is required in order to dispel doubt—trust in the veracity of our own experience gained through meditation and correct observance of practice. It is important to learn that "man proposes but God disposes," and to accept not "my will," but "Thy Will Be Done."

BALANCING THE ENERGIES

Balancing or unblocking the Visuddha chakra energies can result in being:

- consistently calm and contented; centered, independent, and self-referencing
- a good and even inspirational communicator with an authoritative presence and an attractive voice
- truthful and honest at all times
- able to "read between the lines" accurately and hear what has not been said
- musically, poetically, or otherwise creatively inspired
- oriented toward spiritual learning and practice that focuses on realizing eternal Truth

A person who concentrates on the Visuddha chakra, or lotus, can become a great sage, eloquent, and wise. She or he will live a long life, remain free from disease and sorrow, enjoy constant peace of mind, see the past, present, and future, and become the benefactor of all.

Mantra is an integral practice in the clearing and awakening of all the chakras. However, it is a key practice in purifying and awakening the Visuddha chakra in particular, as mantra itself arises from this chakra. Consequently there is more emphasis on mantra practices in the chakra work outlined in this chapter.

WORKBOOK EXERCISES

As with the Muladhara chakra, read carefully through this section and note any physical or psychological energy disorders that may particularly apply to you. Again do this without censoring or judging yourself. Simply note the areas needing attention. After you have read through this section, write down your responses to the following questions in your Workbook Journal.

1. On reading through the physical disorders in the energy blockages section and noting any problems that specifically pertain to you, rate each one on a scale of one to ten in their severity and impact on your life. Also write a paragraph on each disorder, outlining your thoughts and beliefs in relation to its existence and how these have shaped your attitude to managing your discomfort.

2. List eight associations you have with the word "health." As before, do this exercise quickly and without censorship.

3. List eight associations you have with the word "sickness."

4. Write down five areas in your life that need purifying.

5. Write down five associations you have with the word "choice."

6. Name four people you feel you can trust unequivocally.

7. On a scale of one to ten, rate how trustworthy you see yourself.

8. Do you generally follow up on your undertakings? Do you do this quickly or slowly? With each response, list four reasons why you act as you do.

9. On a scale of one to ten, rate how truthful you perceive yourself to be.

10. If there are situations where you are more or less inclined to be truthful, note those situations and list your reasons why.

11. On a scale of one to ten, rate your ability to hold your ground in the face of opposition and/or disapproval. Now note what motivates you in this regard.

12. Make a list of your five strongest attachments.

AWAKENING THE VISUDDHA CHAKRA

In the Visuddha chakra, all the elements of the lower chakras are refined to their purest essence and dissolved in akasha (the void) the element of this chakra. All must be purified in the Visuddha chakra because the upper chakras cannot fully awaken until the awakening of the lower chakras has taken place (with the exception of the Ajna chakra, as discussed previously). Also, the awakening of Shakti Kundalini is not an automatic process, but occurs through Divine Grace according to her timetable, not ours. She cannot be forced and to try to hasten this process is counterproductive and potentially harmful. Each aspect of the system has to be prepared for the high-voltage energy of Kundalini Shakti. Because of this essential purification process, a recommended yoga practice for awakening the Visuddha chakra incorporates the practices for awakening the lower chakras outlined in previous chapters.

AWAKENING THE AJNA CHAKRA

Sit in a stable meditation posture, keeping the spine erect. Place the hands on the knees with the palms up, and bend the index fingers of each hand so that the fingertips touch the base of the thumbs. When you begin to sense the Ajna chakra behind the space between the eyebrows, concentrate on that area from that time onward. Close your eyes and contract and relax the perineum in a natural, unforced, and regular rhythm. Practice this for four to five minutes.

AWAKENING THE MULADHARA CHAKRA

Maintain a stable meditation posture. Interlock the hands and place them below the navel. With your eyes closed, concentrate your eyes and mind on the tip of the nose and breathe normally. Practice this for three to four minutes.

AWAKENING THE SVADISTHANA CHAKRA

Sit in siddha asana or siddha yoni asana, or maintain your usual meditation posture. Press your palms against your knees, lift your shoulders slightly upward and forward, and keep the elbows locked straight. Bend your head down and press your chin firmly against the top of the sternum (see page 77). Close your eyes, keep your body as still as possible, and breathe naturally.

Now concentrate directly on the Svadisthana chakra. Focus on the particular area of your body associated with this chakra and allow your awareness to locate the chakra point in the energy field of your body. While maintaining concentration, slowly contract and relax the muscles in the surrounding area. Begin by contracting and relaxing the chakra point, and slowly expand this area to include the genitals. Ensure that the area of the Muladhara chakra remains relaxed. As before, this practice becomes easier over time. Practice this for three to four minutes.

AWAKENING THE MANIPURA CHAKRA

Remain in siddha asana or siddha yoni asana, or your usual meditation posture. Close your eyes and focus either on the tip of your nose or between the eyebrows. Maintain this focus, keeping your eyes gently closed and the surrounding eye muscles relaxed.

Inhale deeply and imagine the prana in the breath being absorbed through the throat and flowing down to the navel. At the same time, contract the muscles of the rectum and the perineum, and draw them upward. Imagine the pranic energy between the navel and rectum—the apana—flowing up from the Muladhara chakra to the navel.

Hold your breath, concentrate on the navel, and visualize the unification of prana and apana in the navel. Hold this contraction for as long as you can comfortably hold your breath. When you begin to feel pressure to release the breath, release the contraction and then slowly exhale. Practice this for four minutes.

AWAKENING THE ANAHATA CHAKRA

Maintain your meditation posture. With your eyes closed, concentrate on the throat and inhale with full awareness of the incoming breath. Feel the breath filling up the chest cavity—the space around the heart, just above the diaphragm. Remain aware of the contractions and expansions of the heart-space rather than attending to the outgoing breath. Practice for four to five minutes. Allow the image to arise spontaneously.

Finally, while maintaining your meditation posture, concentrate one by one on each chakra ascending from the Muladhara to the Ajna chakra, the sixth chakra. Now reverse the order and concentrate on each chakra descending from the Ajna chakra to the Muladhara chakra.

It may take a little time to become accustomed to this practice, but it does become easier after time. It is also helpful to remind ourselves at certain intervals that to reap the vast reward of spiritual endeavor, we do need commitment and patience.

Cautionary note: Do not force the practice. If at any time you feel physically uncomfortable beyond what you would consider the normal adjustments to a new practice, then stop and concentrate on the other practices for this chakra—particularly the mantra practice, as the Visuddha chakra is particularly connected to mantra and sound.

Continue to note your experiences in your Workbook Journal.

A lovely invocation appropriate to this chakra is the Serenity Prayer:

God grant me the serenity to accept the things I cannot change, courage to change the things I can, and the wisdom to know the difference.

SOUND

Similarly to the sound meditation practices for the lower chakras, this practice comprises intoning the letters—the bija mantras—on the lotus petals of the Visuddha chakra. The letters are **am, am, im, im, um, um, rim, rim, lrim, lrim, em, aim, om, aum, am** (the in-breath—*bindu* and Shiva), and **ah** (the out-breath—*visarga* and Shakti). The Bindu-Visarga is a psychic center between the Ajna and Sahasrara chakras. The letters are pronounced **ang, ang, ing, ing, ung, ung, ring, ring, lring, lring, eng, aing, ong, aung, ang, ahang.**

As with the practices for previous chakras, do this practice by itself until you become accustomed to it and its energy requirements. Be aware of the element akasha while doing the mantra practice. Mantra is a vital practice for the Visuddha chakra.

SOUND MEDITATION

Decide on a time for your meditation practice—say ten minutes in the beginning stages. Adopt your meditation posture or sitting position. Do a few minutes of simple relaxation breathing (page 48) or do simple pranayama practice (page 49) for five rounds.

Concentrate your attention on the hollow area of the lower neck/throat. Intone **ang, ang, ing, ing, ung, ung, ring, ring, lring, lring, eng, aing, ong, aung, ang, ahang** out loud continuously for the duration of the meditation.

At the end of your meditation, sit quietly for a few minutes; notice the energy in and around your body.

Take a few minutes to note the effects of your meditation in your Workbook Journal.

SOUND MEDITATION—MANTRA

In this meditation you continuously repeat the bija mantra of the tattwa of the Visuddha chakra. Be aware of the element akasha while doing the mantra practice. This practice is similar to the sound meditation practice of intoning the letters on the petals of the lotus meditation (see page 137).

The mantra is **ham,** pronounced **hang.** When the sound is correctly articulated, it causes the brain to vibrate and the cerebrospinal fluid to flow more freely into the throat/neck region. This cultivates pleasant and melodious vocal qualities.

When beginning this mantra practice, do it on its own in sitting meditation before combining practices. Decide on a time for your mantra practice—say, ten minutes in the beginning stages. Adopt your meditation asana. Do a few minutes of simple relaxation breathing (page 48) or simple pranayama practice (page 49) for five rounds.

SOUND MEDITATION—MANTRA

Concentrate your attention on the hollow area of the lower neck/throat. The sound **hang** is produced by pushing the air forward and outward from the throat through open lips. Again experiment with different pitches, including G above middle C, and see which pitch feels most comfortable for you in this chakra. Stay with this pitch.

Then intone **hang** out loud continuously for the duration of the meditation. At the end of your meditation, sit quietly for a few minutes; notice the residual sound vibrations, the silence, the energy in and around your body, and how you feel.

Take a few minutes to note the effects of your meditation in your Workbook Journal.

YANTRA

This is a downward-pointing triangle with a white circle and silver crescent within. The triangle has numerous symbolic meanings. Here it represents the past, present, and future; body–mind–spirit; and the Yoni symbol of the feminine energetic principle. It also represents the need to integrate all of these aspects in order to awaken to higher consciousness. The downward-pointing triangle also indicates that when Divine Energy is rightly used and understood, it is available to a greater degree.

The circle represents the shining full moon. The Visuddha chakra is the region of the moon, whereas the Manipura chakra is the region of fire and the Anahata chakra is the region of the sun. This moon is described as pure and stainless, a moon without marks— referring to the visible marks that used to be called the "man in the moon." This lunar region is referred to as the "gateway of the Great Liberation"—for those who have purified and mastered their senses.

The circle also represents the sky, or akasha (void), region. Akasha, the void or space, the element of the Visuddha chakra, is the purest of the elements. All the elements of the lower chakras are dissolved in akasha, which is indicated in the depiction of the circle and the crescent. Akasha is generated by sound. The silver crescent within the circle is also the lunar symbol of **nada** (pure cosmic sound). This is a further symbolic representation in that akasha (the void) is within pure cosmic sound. It is well known in many Eastern spiritual paths that sound, when correctly used and understood—such as in the regular practice of mantra japa—has the capacity to awaken us to our spiritual nature, our eternal true Self.

You may pose a question related to sound and communication in your life at the beginning of the following yantra meditation and visualization. You may also pose questions related to purity and impurities of character, purifying and mastering the senses, opening to psychic ways of knowing, vocal expression, and communication as they relate particularly to your life. As with previous meditations and visualizations, the practice is not one of analytical thought but rather one of staying open to whatever arises.

YANTRA MEDITATION AND VISUALIZATION

When practicing this meditation/visualization, be aware of the element akasha. Being in the presence of this element is said to engender strength, the capacity to become absorbed in deep meditation, the power of clarity in communication, and the direct revelation of knowledge.

Place the image of the yantra where you can see it without strain. Be aware of the hollow space at the base of your throat. Do a few minutes of simple relaxation breathing (page 48) or five rounds of simple pranayama practice (page 49).

Gaze at the yantra and contemplate its form and structure (see page 139). Quietly reflect on the yantra and its symbolism and what arises for you in this space of reflection.

Now contemplate the circle. The Visuddha chakra is the region of the moon. In the yantra, the circle represents the shining full moon. The moon in any aspect indicates paranormal or psychic powers such as clairvoyance, clairaudience, and telepathy. Latent psychic powers awaken when this chakra is purified and awakened. However, the acquisition of these powers is not to be sought as a goal in itself. Like intellectual knowledge, psychic ability can be a trap if desired and utilized for its own sake and for egotistical purposes. Such ability is a side-product of spiritual unfolding and awakening but not the main goal, which is true Self-realization. Spiritual teachings warn against the seduction of intellectual knowledge and heightened powers and of giving these too much attention and thus distracting us from our main spiritual purpose.

The circle also represents the sky, or akasha (void), region. Akasha is generated by sound. As mentioned previously, the Visuddha chakra is where mantra itself arises, hence the practice of mantra is very important in the awakening of this chakra. All of the sound/mantra practices outlined in this chapter can be used in conjunction with visualization of this yantra. Regular practice of mantra japa invokes the power of sound to awaken us to our spiritual nature—our eternal true Self.

WORKBOOK EXERCISES

Reflect on the following and then write down any thoughts, feelings, or insights that arise.

The element of the Visuddha chakra, akasha/ether, is believed to be the element that fills all space. Vibration and sound is related to akasha/ether and the sages of ancient India believed that the field of subtle vibrations pervaded the universe. Everything conceivable in existence reveals the nature of akasha/ether. The elements of the lower chakras—earth, water, fire, and air—are created as manifestations of akasha/ether.

The nature of akasha includes infinite dimensions and permits all possibilities.

Akasha/ether means something very ethereal and elusive. And yet, it is also very powerful. Ethereal is variously defined as light, airy, defying gravity, unsinkable, rarified, fine, wispy, immaterial, delicate, and heavenly. In other words, akasha is a nonmaterial substance of great subtlety.

Now write down your responses to the following questions in your Workbook Journal.
1. List four phenomena that you consider ethereal.
2. List six words you associate with the word "space."
3. Write down three phenomena you associate with vibration.
4. While observing your body, mind, and emotions, repeatedly say no out loud—in different ways and with different intonations—for two minutes. At the end of this time note at least five reactions you noticed. Now repeat this exercise saying yes and note your reactions.
5. When you are in situations that require you to say no or yes, note your reactions and write them down.
6. List six associations you have with the following words: "sound," "speech," "noise."
7. On a scale of one to ten, rate your awareness of personal boundaries—for self and others.
8. Do you need a lot or a little personal space? Why? List your reasons.

DEITIES

ASSOCIATED FEMALE DEITY (FORM OF KUNDALINI): SHAKTI SAKINI

Sakini represents the feminine aspect of Divine Energy manifest and the intelligence on this level. She is the keeper of the door of the Visuddha chakra and, like the Shaktis in the other chakras, is an aspect of Kundalini Shakti. Described as an embodiment of purity whose form is light itself, she is beautiful, radiant, and full of delight, and emanates serenity and peace. The benefactor of higher knowledge and Divine powers, she also represents the bodily substance of bones and is depicted seated on bones.

Sakini is said to reveal much of her teaching to her devotees through dreams. The Visuddha chakra is the center of dreams in the body. The faculties of intuition, inventiveness, memory, spontaneous creativity, and acute wit are all connected to Sakini.

Depicted as half of Shiva's body, Sakini represents the Shakti, the feminine energetic power, of Shiva. At one and the same time, she is the Divine Mother of the Universe and the feminine aspect of the Supreme Lord Shiva.

Sakini has five faces and four arms holding implements. The faces represent the five senses associated with the lower five chakras and their respective elements. She holds a noose, a goad, a bow, and an arrow. These mean, respectively, the entrapment of intellectual knowledge and the seduction of the sound of one's voice, a prompt to further action to attain spiritual goals, a need for preparedness and alertness, and the necessity of clarity of direction. The objects she holds vary in different portrayals. They could include a skull, a rosary, a staff (the goad or noose), and a book (or hand gesture signifying spiritual knowledge). These signify, respectively, worldly detachment, a centering instrument for mantra japa, an implement to control the seduction and arrogance of intellectual knowledge, and spiritual knowledge of the dharma. All of these symbolic instruments and their meanings can be contemplated in meditation.

GODDESS SARASWATI

The Visuddha chakra is also the abode of the revered Devi Saraswati—the Goddess of speech and spiritual knowledge (also called the Goddess of the arts). When Kundalini is activated in this center, Saraswati may awaken Divine powers in a yoga adept, master, or sage that had lain previously dormant. The genuine phenomenon of "speaking in tongues" is an example of this manifestation.

It is also said that when a person has a particularly attractive voice that inspires others, Saraswati has established a connection with that person. Goddess Saraswati is also a form of Shakti, the Divine Mother. Saraswati was also the name of North India's once great river now buried beneath the Thar Desert.

MEDITATION ON SHAKTI SAKINI

Meditation on the deities of the Visuddha chakra begins with Shakti Sakini and continues with Sadashiva. Again, be aware of the presence of the element akasha to enhance the meditation and to assist in developing beneficial qualities. Sakini is the doorkeeper of the Visuddha chakra; her form is described as light itself. She is depicted as beautiful, radiant, full of delight, and an embodiment of purity emanating peace and serenity. The faculties of intuition, inventiveness, memory, spontaneous creativity, and acute wit are all connected to Sakini.

Decide on a definite time for your meditation—try to allow at least twenty minutes in the beginning. Include relaxation breathing time and notation time at the end.

Place a picture of Sakini where it can be seen without strain or practice internal concentration on the qualities of Sakini in the hollow space at the base of the throat/neck. Assume meditation posture. Begin with a few minutes of simple relaxation breathing (page 48) or five rounds of simple pranayama practice (page 49). As you breathe, be aware of the air flowing into your nostrils and into the space in the throat. Concentrate on the hollow space at the base of your throat.

Meditate on Sakini as the door-keeper to the Visuddha chakra, and focus on the qualities of Sakini as described on page 142. Be mindful of Sakini as a Goddess protector and benefactor bestowing higher knowledge and Divine powers. Be aware also that Sakini reveals her knowledge and teachings through dreams. Reflect on the symbolic meanings of the implements she holds, as outlined on page 142.

At the end of your meditation, sit quietly for a few minutes. Notice the energies in and around your body and how you feel.

Make a note of your meditation experience in your Workbook Journal.

ASSOCIATED MALE DEITY: SADASHIVA

Sadashiva is a composition of all the Shiva energies. He represents the intelligence on this level and the masculine aspect of Divine Energy unmanifest. Sadashiva is depicted as clothed in a tiger skin and wearing a garland of snakes. He has five heads, each with three eyes, and ten arms holding various objects. The heads represent the five essential principles (sound, smell, taste, form, and touch) and the five elements that evolved from them, and also signify the higher qualities of omnipresence, omniscience, and omnipotence, and the sublimation of the five senses. The third eye in each face represents higher wisdom.

The ten arms and their objects indicate efficiency. The garland of snakes represents power used with wisdom. One hand is held in a mudra for dispelling fears and granting fearlessness. He also holds symbolic objects: a noose—a warning and a tool for reining in the pride and arrogance that often accompanies the acquisition of intellectual knowledge; a goad—a prompt for further action to attain spiritual goals; a battle-ax—to sever old personality aspects; a bell—symbol of listening and for attentiveness; a trident—symbol of the Hindu Trinity and the physical, etheric, and causal bodies; a sword—for discrimination; fire—the fire of ambition and aspiration; the snake king (*Ngendra*)—symbolizing wisdom or temptation; and a diamond scepter—symbolizing awareness of power. All of these symbolic objects and their meanings can be contemplated in meditation. All the elements have dissolved into one in Sadashiva. The earth element has dissolved into water, which has been dissolved into fire, which has dissolved into air, which has dissolved into the void, or akasha—the element of the Visuddha chakra—and all the elements in their essence are united in Sadashiva in the Visuddha chakra. As this chakra is purified, we become aware of the limitations of the elements and the human plane of existence.

MEDITATION ON SADASHIVA

Sadashiva is composed of all the Shiva energies. All the elements have dissolved into one and are united in Sadashiva. As this chakra is purified, we become aware of the limitations of the elements and the human plane of existence.

Decide on a time for your meditation. Try to allow at least twenty minutes. Include relaxation breathing time and notation time at the end.

Place a picture of Sadashiva where you can easily see it without strain or meditate on the qualities of Sadashiva in the hollow space at the base of your throat. Adopt your meditation posture. Begin with a few minutes of simple relaxation breathing (page 48) or five rounds of simple pranayama practice (page 49). Be aware of the air flowing in through your nostrils and into the space of your throat. Concentrate your attention on the hollow space at the base of the throat.

Begin your meditation practice by focusing on a picture of Sadashiva and/or on his qualities, as mentioned on page 145. In this meditation Sadashiva can be visualized or contemplated upon as the Master Teacher within. Be aware also of the symbolic meanings of the implements Sadashiva holds. Attaining balance of all the bodily elements brings centeredness and the bliss of nondual consciousness.

When you become familiar with Sadashiva, instead of focusing on a pictorial representation, try to invoke his presence in your mind's eye. Also continue to focus on the qualities symbolized by Sadashiva. It is said that through meditating on Sadashiva, we will be released from the past and all karmas, and the consciousness will be reborn in recognition of the Oneness of Being. The awareness of eternal knowledge is realized when the focus of all energies ascends to the Ajna chakra.

At the end of your meditation, allow yourself to sit quietly for a few minutes. Notice the energies in and around your body and how you feel.

THE BINDU-VISARGA AND THE MANTRA SO'HAM

The psychic center between the Ajna chakra and the Sahasrara chakra is called the Bindu-Visarga, also known as the Bindu chakra or Chandra chakra (moon center). The Visuddha chakra is closely connected to the Bindu-Visarga, which produces nectar that is not yet assimilated by the body as it is burned up by the element fire in the Manipura chakra. The practices for the Bindu-Visarga are designed to control the nectar this center produces. The Bindu-Visarga is activated by devout Hindu practitioners in a number of ways. One practice—observable in photographs of Indian saddhus (holy men) and dedicated yoga practitioners—is by growing a tuft of hair on the crown of the head. This tuft is pulled into a tight bun close to the scalp, and this exerts a tug that draws the attention to this spot.

Another practice is the yoga exercise called *kechari mudra*, which consists of rolling the tongue backward so that the underside of the tongue touches the back of the palate. Although this is a relatively simple practice, in its beginning stages it must be done correctly and needs monitoring under expert guidance as the practice progresses.

Another practice is the repetition of the mantra **So'Ham,** or **Sa'Ham.** Yoga adepts who have a refined awareness of the breath are able to hear the internal sound of **So'Ham,** which means "I Am He." **Sa'Ham** means "I Am She." Both essentially mean "I Am That." Regular practice of this mantra establishes a rhythm in harmony with all of the life-force around you. The **ham** of the mantra is pronounced **hang.**

When you begin this practice, use your fingers to count and to keep a regular rhythm. In time, the rhythm will flow naturally and you will no longer need to use finger counting.

SO'HAM MEDITATION

Adopt your meditation posture. Do a few minutes of simple relaxation breathing (page 48), or five rounds of simple pranayama practice (page 49).

Inhale and on the exhalation mentally say **so** or **sa.**
Inhale and mentally say **hang (ham)**.
Exhale and mentally repeat **so** or **sa.**
Inhale and mentally repeat **hang (ham)**.

Repeat the mantra for four to five minutes and then reverse the pattern:
Exhale and mentally say **hang (ham)** on the exhalation.
Inhale and mentally say **so** or **sa.**
Repeat this mantra for four to five minutes.

At the end of the practice, sit quietly for a moment or two. Notice the energy in and around your body and how you feel.

Note the effects of the practice in your Workbook Journal. As you progress with this practice, you may wish to increase the time you take—if and when it feels natural to do so. In time, a result of this practice can be the experience of an immense inner stillness.

WORKBOOK EXERCISES—REVIEW

At this stage of your journey, it is important to review your progress so far. Go through your Workbook Journal and appraise your work with the four lower chakras. You will be able to do this by looking at the changes that have occurred within you and at your present state of being. It is very important to have clarity regarding the Visuddha chakra, which comes about through the purification of body–mind–emotions–speech. Ask yourself the following questions and note your answers in your Workbook Journal.

1. List ten things that you notice have changed positively as a result of your chakra work in your physical, mental, and emotional being, and in your relationships.
2. List five areas in your inner and outer life that appear resistant to change and that you perceive still need clearing and purifying.
3. Note what else arises in the course of your appraisal.

The Visuddha chakra is connected to the sense of hearing. Note your responses to these questions:

4. On a scale of one to ten, rate how attentive a listener you perceive yourself to be. Then rate how effectively you believe you communicate.
5. On a scale of one to ten, rate how absorbed/distracted you become in listening to your thoughts.
6. List five expressions of nonverbal communication.
7. On a scale of one to ten, rate your ability to listen to and act on intuition or inner guidance.

The Visuddha chakra is also the center of dreams in the body. From now on, keep a separate Dream Diary and record your dreams and see what they have to reveal.

Remember: The Visuddha chakra is the "gateway of the Great Liberation" for those who have mastered their senses by having worked through and purified the four lower chakras and their related elements.

CHAPTER NINE

THE AJNA CHAKRA

Where is the sixth chakra located? How do you awaken this chakra through meditation on sound, mantra, yantra, and its deities? Review your journey so far.

Ajna is the sixth chakra, or lotus. The Sanskrit name means "command" or "command wheel." The Ajna chakra is the command center of the chakras. It is also known as the Brow chakra or Third-eye chakra. The Ajna chakra is the place of meditation and the seat of spiritual knowledge.

Location A point midway between the eyebrows—in the brain core.

Tattwa/Element *Mahatattva*—in which all other elements are present in their pure essence. The elements associated with the lower chakras are refined to their purest essence and dissolved into ether. This happens by purification of the elements. In the Ajna chakra we have moved beyond the five material elements of earth, water, fire, air, and akasha/ether.

Color White or bluish-white. In the West, commonly depicted as violet or indigo.

Lotus A luminous white circle with two white petals. The two petals and the enclosing circle of the lotus represent three qualities: *sattva* (purity and light); *rajas* (passion and activity); and *tamas* (darkness and inertia). The two petals are also symbolic of the functioning of *manas* (the mind) in the two worlds of reality—the manifest and the unmanifest. They also represent the Ida and Pingala Nadis, which unite in the Ajna chakra and also terminate in their respective nostrils.

Letters on the Lotus Petals Ham, ksham. **Ham** represents the final opening up of creation, and **ksham** is the letter that includes all of the other letters of the Sanskrit alphabet. This indicates that we have come to the end of the manifestation of the phenomenal universe.

Seed Sound/Bija Mantra OM—AUM.

Vehicle of the Seed Sound Nada—pure cosmic sound—in the form of a crescent.

Associated Plexus and Glands Medulla plexus, pineal and pituitary glands.

Associated Female Deity Shakti Hakini.

Associated Male Deity Shambu/Paramashiva or Ardhanarishvara.

Associated Parts of the Body The brain and neurological system; pituitary and pineal glands; eyes, ears, and nose.

Ruling Planet Saturn.

Associated Astrological Signs and Planets in Western Astrology Capricorn and Saturn; Aquarius and Uranus; Pisces and Neptune; Sagittarius and Jupiter; Mercury.

CHARACTERISTICS

The aspect of the Ajna chakra is Self-realization—Unity Consciousness. All ideas, interests, and desires—all energies—are directed toward absorption in the Divine Energy. The Ajna chakra is the boundary between human and Divine Consciousness. It is associated with mind (*manas*) and the sense of individuality, or ego (*ahamkara*). Mind in this instance includes the conscious, subconscious, and unconscious mind, the intellect, and ego.

The Ajna chakra involves our abilities and skills in reasoning with clarity and in evaluating our attitudes and beliefs. It is the "third-eye" center, which represents the ability to "know" through nonordinary means—through intuition, psychic abilities, insight, and wisdom. It involves the courage of learning to act on inner direction and perception and standing firm in inner resolve. This chakra challenges us to:

- open the mind
- develop detachment from personal and material concerns
- become finely attuned to our true motivations
- confront our remaining fears and illusions
- refine our ability to distinguish the authentic and inauthentic
- speak the truth always and surrender to the inner power of Divine Truth rather than externally imposed "truths"

The Ajna chakra is about developing and realizing an imperturbable inner equanimity so that there is no further conflict between what is "inside" and what is "outside." It is also about recognizing that in actuality there really is no boundary between them, that All is One.

ENERGY BLOCKAGES

Unbalanced or blocked Ajna chakra energies can manifest as single or multiple disorders that indicate either a deficiency or excess of energy in this center.

PHYSICAL DISORDERS

This chakra influences the brain and neurological system, the pituitary and pineal glands, and the eyes, ears, and nose. Consequently, some of the physical problems that can occur are headaches, migraines, eye problems, nightmares and/or disturbing visions, sinus problems such as sinusitis, catarrh, and hay fever, hormonal imbalances, insomnia, and certain allergies.

PSYCHOLOGICAL DISORDERS

These may include weak concentration—inability to focus on one thing; feeling out of touch with the body and/or "out of it"—out of balance, psychically disturbed; mental tension; little insight and discrimination between surface appearances of reality and true reality, leading to confusion about what is real and what is not; and lack of congruence between the actuality of our experiences and what we profess and believe to be real. Other disorders include feelings of inadequacy and hypersensitivity to the projected feelings or opinions of others; hiding behind intellectual knowledge and analysis; being manipulative, egocentric, dogmatic, proud, or, conversely, timid and hesitant; and being unable to distinguish between the personal self and the higher Self.

BALANCING THE ENERGIES

When the Ajna chakra energies are unblocked, this can manifest as:
- detachment from material possessions
- unconcern about the ego desires for ambition, fame, wealth, or gain
- being at ease in any situation in life
- contentment; being a neutral witness of life yet compassionate in attitude
- clean and clear forgiveness
- a greater ability to live fully in the present, in the now, and flow with the rhythm of life

Other attainments are:
- clarity of perception
- reliable intuition
- true discrimination
- realized psychic powers such as clairvoyance, clairaudience, telepathy, astral travel, and access to the past lives of self and others
- the ability to see energy within, around, and beyond material form
- being spiritually responsible with personal powers

To have reached the Ajna chakra shows a high level of spiritual attainment, the level of a yogi or yogini with considerable psychic powers. This attainment also carries the responsibility to be of spiritual service to others on the spiritual path.

WORKBOOK EXERCISES

As with the Muladhara chakra, read carefully through this section and note down any physical or psychological energy disorders that may particularly apply to you. Again do this without censoring or judging yourself. Simply note the areas needing attention.

1. After reading through the physical areas and disorders associated with this chakra, note any disorders that particularly relate to you, your beliefs about these, and courses of redress.
2. List six associations you have with the following words: "mind," "intelligence," "intellect," and "ego." As before, do this exercise quickly and honestly.
3. Is there any discrepancy between your values and goals and actions? If so, list each one.
4. List five associations you have with the words "surrender" and "humility."
5. Write a paragraph on how you now see death.
6. Is there any incongruence between your self-perception and the feedback you receive from others? If so, note each area and the emotions this elicits in you.
7. On a scale of one to ten, rate your ability to sustain one-pointed concentration.
8. List your attachments at this point.
9. Write a paragraph on your definition of "reality."
10. List three areas that give rise to resistance in you.
11. On a scale of one to ten, rate your ability to be present in any given moment.
12. Is there any area within yourself and/or in your relationships with others that still needs forgiveness? If so, list them, open to guidance, and note what arises.
13. On a scale of one to ten, rate your feelings of inner contentment.
14. List ten things in life for which you feel gratitude.

TRATAKA—MEDITATION FOR AWAKENING THE AJNA CHAKRA

This is a practice for awakening the Third-eye chakra. Its other benefits include developing the power of concentration necessary for true meditation and calming the mind. It helps relieve mental tension and insomnia and improve the eyesight. The eyes are the windows to the mind and soul, and when the gaze is steady, the mind becomes stable and ultimately free of thoughts.

Have a lighted candle facing you at eye level, about one to two feet away from your sitting position. Dim the room and adopt your meditation posture. Keep your spine erect. Close your eyes; do a few minutes of simple relaxation breathing (page 48). Once your body is in a comfortable position and relaxed, remain still for the duration of the practice.

Open your eyes and attempt to gaze steadily, without blinking, at the bright part of the flame just above the tip of the wick. Your gaze needs to be fixed intently on that one point. Hold the gaze until your eyes begin to water.

Now close your eyes and concentrate internally, with your inner vision, on the afterimage of the flame. Try to hold the image just in front of the center of the eyebrows. When the image begins to fade, open your eyes and again gaze at the candle flame until your eyes water. Close the eyes and again concentrate on the afterimage until it begins to fade. Repeat this process for about fifteen to twenty minutes.

With repeated practice it becomes possible to gaze at the candle flame without blinking or moving the eyeballs. Also, you can lose awareness of the body during the practice. Trataka is of immense benefit to visualization and meditation practice because of its power to develop one-pointed concentration. It also develops latent psychic ability, particularly clairvoyance. Working with the simple purity of a candle flame also serves to remind us of the light that shines continuously within us.

SOUND

This practice comprises intoning the letters on the lotus petals **ham, ksham.** These are pronounced **hang, kshang.** Meditation and mantra practice on the seed sounds of the petals **ham, ksham (hang, kshang)** activate the sound units that are connected with three of the finer nadis in the Sushumna Nadi. **Ham** represents the final opening up of creation, and **ksham** is the letter that includes all of the other letters of the Sanskrit alphabet.

SOUND MEDITATION

Decide on a time for your sound meditation practice—say, five to ten minutes in the beginning. Adopt your meditation posture or sitting position. Do a few minutes of simple relaxation breathing (page 48) or simple pranayama practice (page 49) for five rounds.

Experiment with pitches, including A above middle C, and find the pitch that feels most comfortable. Now intone **hang, kshang** out loud, and do so continuously for the duration of the meditation.

At the end of your meditation, sit quietly for a few minutes; notice the silence and the energy in and around your body.

Note your experiences in your Workbook Journal.

MANTRA PRACTICE—OM

The primal cosmic sound, **anahata nada,** is present everywhere and is more commonly known as "white noise." This "auspicious humming sound" arising from vibration begins in the Heart chakra as OM (A-U-M)—also known as the *pranava*—the source of all sounds. **OM** is the bija mantra of the Ajna chakra. It is an approximation of the "unstruck" sound heard internally by yogis and those adept at meditation. The refined sound frequencies of OM vibrate and emanate from within those who have eliminated all negativities and impurities. OM is also recognized as the quintessential mantra. Today, as in the past, the true believer who seeks transcendence and union with the Divine through sound faithfully chants the mantra OM within the quiet of her or his own heart and mind. OM recurs in all of the major religions: to Christians and Jews as Amen; to Muslims as Amin; and to Hindus, Buddhists, and Jains as OM (AUM).

The mantra OM is sounded as **a-u-m.** The "m" is sounded nasally. OM is a combination of sun (A), moon (U), and fire (M). It represents creation, preservation, and destruction; the life-force; the universal sound; and the unity of all sound.

OM MEDITATION

Adopt siddha asana or siddha yoni asana, padma asana, or other meditation posture. Ensure the spine is erect. Once you have found a comfortable position, keep the body still. Close your eyes and focus on the space between your eyebrows.

Practice a few minutes of simple relaxation breathing (page 48) and release all tension on the out breath. Inhale deeply into your abdomen and begin to sound **a–u–m.** Pronounce the first part of the sound as a long "a" (as in a-a-a or ah-ah-ah) and allow the sound to vibrate in the abdomen around the navel area.

Now pronounce the second part of the sound as a long "u" (as in o-o-o), moving the breath and attention to the chest area. Allow the sound to vibrate in the middle of the chest—the Anahata chakra or spiritual heart center.

Pronounce the third part of the sound as a long "m-m-m" with a nasal resonance (like ng), moving your focus to the nasal passages and to the area between your eyebrows— the Ajna chakra area—and allow the sound to vibrate in your "third eye."

After the full exhalation of sound, again take a deep breath into the abdomen. Repeat the mantra process as above. Feel the ascension of the sound and the vibrations throughout your body. Continue for at least ten minutes—or twelve rounds—if you are able.

Note your experiences in your Workbook Journal.

YANTRA

Inside the circle of the white lotus with two petals is the yantra of a golden downward-pointing triangle and the sacred syllable of the mantra **OM (AUM)**. The golden triangle is symbolic of the workings of Divine Energy in its pure state and in its manifest state. Within the triangle is the Yoni—symbol of the feminine—with a Shiva Lingam called Itara Lingam in the center of the circle. This represents the Divine Union, which gives birth to the cosmos and Cosmic Consciousness.

ITARA LINGAM

The white Shiva Lingam known as *Itara Lingam* in the center of the circle is the third lingam of the chakras, and it has the bija mantra **OM (AUM)**. Itara Shiva, represented by the lingam, controls the subtle mind, which is beyond the modus operandi of the senses. These are located in the first five chakras. Consequently, Itara Shiva has complete control over elemental desires. The Itara Lingam is described as luminescent white, with streaks of lightning, which represent power and energy. It is also the site of **Rudra Granthi,** the third and last of the knots that have to be untied on the path of liberation.

YANTRA MEDITATION AND VISUALIZATION

In meditating on this yantra, reflect on the potential sense of completion represented by the circle. When this chakra is pure and awakened, the goal of the union of the human and the Divine in blissful Self-realization is within reach. The journey has been long and arduous, with many moments of joy and pain, laughter and tears, despair and exhilaration, as we face what we have been and as we come close to knowing our true nature—who we really are—and the ultimate purpose of our human existence. Perhaps there have been fleeting but unforgettable experiences of the blissful Self—glimpses to keep us going and to show us the eternal bliss that awaits us.

DEITIES

ASSOCIATED FEMALE DEITY (FORM OF KUNDALINI): SHAKTI HAKINI

Shakti Hakini is the keeper of the door to the Ajna chakra. She represents the aspect of the union of Divine Energy manifest and unmanifest. The intelligence on this level is symbolized in unity—Shiva and Shakti are in union in the Ajna chakra. Hakini also represents the substance of marrow.

Hakini has six heads—Kundalini has gained an additional head with each chakra, which indicates that the mind (*manas*) has expanded in subtlety and power. Her four (or sometimes six) hands indicate a high degree of efficiency. The heads represent undivided concentration, unhindered meditation, superconscious awareness, and enlightenment.

Hakini holds a spiritual tool in each hand. A drum indicates the rhythm of life, that life continues, and that we have a responsibility to share spiritual knowledge with others. It also represents pure cosmic sound and the power of sound to awaken higher consciousness. One hand is in a mudra to dispel fears; another hand holds a skull—symbol of advanced mental powers and worldly detachment. The remaining hand holds a mala to use as a centering device. It is also a reminder of past lives in that each bead represents a former life whose influence has brought us to our present state of being, and that our work in this life determines our future karmic destiny. Hakini may also display a gesture for granting blessings and boons, or hold a book representing retention of knowledge or a staff with a skull on top, signifying the attainment of a mind with unexpectedly awesome powers, which, when exercised with intuition, will be utilized beneficially for others.

MEDITATION ON SHAKTI HAKINI

Meditating on Hakini is said to help us attain all essential qualities and powers for working in the Ajna chakra and allow us to experience the presence of nectar that flows from the Kamadhenu, the wish-fulfilling cow, which is in the Soma chakra.

As with previous meditations, place a picture of Hakini where you can see it without strain or meditate internally on the symbolism of Hakini and the instruments she holds and their meanings. Follow the basic meditation procedures for the deities in previous chapters. As the Shakti works in this chakra, the mind stabilizes and becomes quiet and pure. Meditation now comes naturally and spontaneously.

ASSOCIATED MALE DEITY: SHAMBU (ALSO CALLED PARAMASHIVA) OR ARDHANARISHVARA

Shambu/Paramashiva is the form of Shiva in his highest aspect. In some texts, Ardhanarishvara is depicted as the deity of the Ajna chakra. This form is half female—Shakti—and half male—Shiva—and symbolizes the fundamental "unity in polarity" of male–female, lunar–solar, left–right, and light–dark. This also represents the formless reality that is Shiva, and that which manifests form that is Shakti; and their Divine union into One Being. This indicates a transcendence of duality.

Ardhanarishvara

MEDITATION ON SHAMBU/PARAMASHIVA OR ARDHANARISHVARA

When you are meditating on Shambu/Paramashiva, or Ardhanarishvara, regard him as the great inner teacher and guide. Or contemplate the third-eye center that is the Ajna chakra and open to the guidance of inner wisdom emanating from this chakra.

Place a picture of Shambu/Paramashiva (Shiva in his highest aspect) or Ardhanarishvara (Shiva as half male and half female—Shakti) where you can easily see it without strain and/or meditate on the qualities of these symbolized forms of Shiva as outlined earlier. Adopt your meditation posture. Begin with a few minutes of simple relaxation breathing (page 48) or five rounds of simple pranayama practice (page 49). Be aware of the air flowing in through your nostrils. Concentrate your attention on the space between the eyebrows.

Begin your meditation practice by focusing on the image of Shambu/Paramashiva or Ardhanarishvara, and/or meditate on the qualities of these forms of Shiva. When you become familiar with Shambu/Paramashiva or Ardhanarishvara, instead of focusing on a pictorial representation, try to invoke his presence in your mind's eye. Also continue to focus on the qualities symbolized by these forms of Shiva.

When meditating on Shambu/Paramashiva or Ardhanarishvara, also be mindful of the state of masculine and feminine energies within you at this point and the necessity of integrating these energies. This means being inner-directed and independent, becoming complete in yourself, without the need to have anyone else to complement or to compensate you for aspects you perceive to be lacking in yourself. This requires the courage to stand firm on the basis of true inner experience rather than conceptualized or externalized belief. Discrimination is also essential—to distinguish between being motivated by true intuition and spiritual aspiration, or by ego or fear.

Note your experiences in your Workbook Journal.

SELF-INQUIRY MEDITATION

This is an opportune time to ask again, "Who am I?" This is the driving question we asked at the beginning of our journey. This one question, the ultimate question, is the basis of a traditional Hindu Vedanta practice called *Vichara Marga,* the path of Self-inquiry.

The purpose of Self-inquiry is to experience the revelation of the true Self, not to probe mentally or seek a definitive answer. The revelation of the Self is experienced beyond words, but we *know* without any doubt the veracity of this experience when it occurs. The practice is simple but not easy, and requires commitment and consistent practice to reap the incomparable bliss it bestows.

Essentially, this is a practice of simply and repeatedly asking yourself the question, **"Who am I?"** and holding this thought alone, with a mind that is completely open and receptive to any responses or sensations that may arise.

In the beginning, practice this for twenty minutes. As you progress in this practice, you can extend the time to thirty to sixty minutes or longer.

Adopt your preferred meditation posture. Ensure your spine is straight, with your head and neck in alignment. Once you are comfortable, keep your body still for the duration of the practice. Close your eyes and practice a few minutes of simple relaxation breathing (page 48), releasing all tension on the out breath.

Focus your attention in the middle of your chest in the spiritual Heart center. Inwardly and quietly and with an open mind and heart, ask yourself "Who am I?" without demanding or expecting a response. Maintain your focus of attention on the Heart center and breathe naturally. When thoughts arise, do not pursue them or be captivated by them, but simply inquire of each thought, "To whom has this thought arisen?" If the answer comes "To me," then repeat the question "Who am I?" From time to time, repeat the question in a relaxed way, without any expectation of an answer.

WORKBOOK EXERCISES—REVIEW

Note your experiences of the Self-inquiry meditation in your Workbook Journal. Even when you seem to experience little or feel only impatience and frustration, write this down. All is a seed for potential transformation.

When your practice has reached the Ajna chakra, it is a time for re-evaluation. This reassessment applies whether you began your chakra-clearing work at the Muladhara chakra or the Ajna chakra and then moved to the Muladhara chakra, working sequentially upward.

1. Reflect on your passage through the chakras and dispassionately review your present state of being in relation to where you were when you began this journey. This process requires complete honesty in deep reflection and meditation. Also write down your responses to the following questions in your Workbook Journal.
2. Note what fears you still experience and the particular times when these fears arise.
3. On a scale of one to ten, rate your ability to accept—not just tolerate—differences in all areas of life.
4. List five ways you demonstrate an ability to openly cooperate with others.
5. On a scale of one to ten, rate your ability to empathize with others.
6. Rate the degree to which you feel able to calmly hold your ground in the face of rejection, disapproval, ridicule, and/or coercion.
7. Write down five ways in which you demonstrate a clear ability to follow your intuition.
8. On a scale of one to ten, rate your degree of self-acceptance and your ability to be compassionate toward others and yourself.

At this level we begin to see each face of any phenomenon and the purpose of each polarity to reflect its opposite, to live comfortably in the paradox, and to experience the All in One and One in All.

CHAPTER TEN

THE SAHASRARA CHAKRA

Learn about the seventh, or Crown, chakra and its characteristics. Where is the seventh chakra located? What does it mean to attain enlightenment or Self-realization? Practice the OM mantra meditation and visualization of White Light. Review your journey through the chakras.

Sahasrara is the seventh chakra, or lotus. The Sanskrit name means "one thousand," "thousand-spoke wheel," or "thousand-petaled"—referring to the thousand petals of this supreme lotus. It is also known as the Crown chakra. The Sahasrara chakra is the seat of the **Parama Hamsah** (Supreme Self). The Sahasrara chakra is different from the other chakras in that it is the realm of ultimate Truth, ultimate reality—the realm of pure Consciousness. The traditional texts speak of the piercing of only six chakras, which is why many schools of Kundalini Yoga account for only six chakras—with the Sahasrara chakra referred to as the seat of pure Consciousness.

Location Crown of the head.

Color Colorless or white, with lotus petals the colors of the rainbow spectrum. In the West, this chakra is often said to be the color violet.

Lotus Colorless or lustrous white and "radiant like the cool rays of the full moon." A thousand petals, turned downward, of the variegated colors of the rainbow are arranged in rows of twenty according to the fifty letters of the Sanskrit alphabet. Some texts say the petals are tinged with the "gold of the rising sun." Each petal in each row carries a letter of the Sanskrit alphabet, constituting twenty rows of the Sanskrit alphabet. The Sahasrara chakra is closely connected to the Soma chakra and the A-Ka-Tha Triangle within that chakra. In the sacred texts the Sahasrara chakra is frequently called the region of sun, moon, and fire—a reference to the A-Ka-Tha Triangle. The first line of the Triangle is the line of fire, the element considered to be the origin of life, and as such is associated with Brahma the Creator. The second line is the line of the moon, connected with preservation and associated with Vishnu the Preserver. The third line is the line of the sun, which symbolizes the twelve suns that rise up to burn the world at the time of dissolution, so it is associated with Rudra, a form of Shiva (deity of the Manipura chakra). The A-Ka-Tha Triangle is also the abode of Kundalini Shakti—as Kashevari—and Paramashiva—as Kameshvara—as the guru within, the Supreme Guru.

Letters on the Lotus Petals All fifty letters of the Sanskrit alphabet—the sounds of all the Sanskrit vowels and consonants—and "all pure sounds from Ah to Ksha."

Vehicle of the Seed Sound Bindu—the dot above the crescent, the primordial point of cosmic emergence, the point of origin of all beginnings and all dissolutions. This is the visual equivalent of OM, the seed symbol of sound. The bija mantra of this chakra is said by some to be a specific breathing sound in the pronunciation of Sanskrit, called *visarga*.

Associated Plexus and Glands Cerebral plexus.

Associated Parts of the Body Central nervous system, skin, muscular system.

Yantra In some texts, said to be a circle symbolizing a full moon; in others, said to be formless.

CHARACTERISTICS

A person who has reached the Sahasrara chakra has transcended the realms of animal and human consciousness. When the consciousness is stabilized she or he becomes one with pure Consciousness—there is no longer any separate individuality. It is in the Sahasrara chakra that we realize the Oneness of the individual soul and the Supreme Soul. The illusion of *jiva* (an individual self) is dissolved. Once the Kundalini Shakti rushes through the Ajna chakra to the higher chakra, the full release of its energy is certain.

SELF-REALIZATION

As Kundalini Shakti rises through the chakras, she absorbs all the elements, the tattwas, into herself. The element earth and its predominant sense of smell in the Muladhara chakra dissolve into the element water at the Svadisthana chakra; the element water and its predominant sense of taste are absorbed into the fire element at the Manipura chakra; the fire element and its predominant sense of sight merge into akasha/ether at the Visuddha chakra; ether and its predominant sense of hearing are absorbed into the mind and other psychic faculties at the Ajna chakra; and finally the mind dissolves into the Self at the Sahasrara chakra. This state of Being transcends the brain and the nervous system. The psycho-physical constitution is permanently altered. It is a state beyond thought and beyond the reaches of the ego. It is a "wordless" state of pure knowledge, an expanded state of Consciousness difficult to communicate in the container of words, which are only ever an approximation of experience in any case.

THE SOMA CHAKRA OR LOTUS

Above the Ajna chakra, within the Sahasrara (seventh) chakra, is a minor but very important chakra—the Soma chakra. This lotus has twelve or sixteen petals with a triangle, the A-Ka-Tha Triangle, and a crescent moon within the lotus circle. The moon is the source of nectar for the body, which it receives from the wish-fulfilling cow, Kamadhenu, and three nadis. The nectar is constantly oozing from the hollow space between the twin hemispheres of the brain, known as "the cave of the bumble bee."

The nectar normally flows down to the Manipura chakra, where it is burned up in the digestive fire. Through practices such as meditation and *kechari mudra* (see page 147), Kundalini Yoga practitioners who have pierced the third and final "knot," the Rudra Granthi, and learned to control the flow of nectar, attain the bliss of eternal union with the Divine.

KAMESHVARA CHAKRA

A little above the Soma chakra is another minor chakra or lotus within the Sahasrara chakra, called the Kameshvara chakra. It is of the utmost significance. It is in this chakra that Kundalini Shakti, in the form of Kameshvari, described as the most beautiful female in the three worlds (*Tripura Sundari*), is united with Lord Shiva as Kameshvara, the most beautiful of all male forms. When Kundalini Shakti is aroused through various yoga practices, she rushes upward to meet and unite with her Lord. In flowing upward, she turns up all the petals of all the lotuses, the chakras, which had previously been turned downward, and absorbs all aspects of the individual consciousness and the phenomenal world. At this time, the chakras become inactive. When Shakti Kundalini as Kashevari unites with Lord Shiva as Kameshvara—that is, Supreme Consciousness—Truth, goodness, and beauty that arise from knowing, doing, and feeling are realized, and integrated into all forms of behavior and expression.

KUNDALINI'S JOURNEY HOME

Unlike most popular literature on the subject, the scriptures tell us that Kundalini Shakti's rise to the Sahasrara chakra is not necessarily a one-time phenomenon. On the contrary, she usually returns to the Muladhara chakra at the base of the spine. Some say Kundalini Shakti remains in union with Shiva, the Self, for a while, and then descends to the Muladhara chakra, restoring the powers and the deities of the chakras on her descent. When she reaches the Muladhara chakra, Kundalini Shakti coils up again. However, the person is said to be permanently changed, living out her or his karmas in an expanded state of consciousness, and upon death is in complete union with pure Consciousness. Other texts say that Kundalini Shakti repeatedly returns to the Muladhara chakra or remains in the upper chakras until such time as she becomes stabilized in the Sahasrara chakra. When this happens, she does not return—the union is complete.

Other accounts on Kundalini Shakti and the chakras, such as that given by the great sage Sri Bhagavan Ramana Maharshi, tell us that even when the Kundalini Shakti reaches the Sahasrara chakra, this does not result in Self-realization. For final realization, he says, "the Kundalini must go beyond the Sahasrara, down another *nadi* called *amritanadi*…and into the Heart-center."

Ultimately, Self-realization occurs after perhaps many lifetimes of dedicated spiritual practice in preparation for the final awakening, which happens seemingly spontaneously and only through Divine Grace.

ENLIGHTENMENT AND SELF-REALIZATION

It is often said and written that enlightenment is the ultimate state of Being. However, enlightenment is not necessarily the ultimate liberation (moksha) or Self-realization. From ultimate liberation there is no return to a separate human consciousness, but in enlightenment there can still be a residual duality of consciousness and interplay between human and Divine Consciousness, albeit in the higher chakras.

The important aspect of all these accounts is to realize that the bliss or ecstasy we may experience in meditation, the expanded states of altered consciousness we may periodically experience, or the psychic powers we may develop are not in themselves indications of ultimate spiritual attainment—the realization of pure Consciousness. However, these experiences do tell us that Self-realization only occurs on the higher planes of existence, which necessitates the purification of the lower planes, and that spiritual attainment is unattainable without dedicated life-long practice.

ENERGY BLOCKAGES

Unbalanced or blocked Sahasrara chakra energies can manifest as single or multiple disorders that indicate either a deficiency or excess of energy in this center.

ON THE PHYSICAL LEVEL

Disorders may include migraines, brain disorders or diseases, nervous-system disorders, and physical symptoms or ailments without apparent physical cause.

ON THE PSYCHO-SPIRITUAL LEVEL

These may include alienation, apathy, frustration, indecision, self-consciousness, and superiority and abuse of power, especially to those considered to be inferior and "lesser life forms." Other manifestations are spiritual doubt and/or denial of spiritual reality, or religious fanaticism of one form or another, such as fundamentalism or sectarianism.

BALANCING THE ENERGIES

When the Sahasrara chakra energies are balanced or unblocked, this can manifest as Self-realization. The illuminated state of Self-realization also manifests as a radiant aura around the person. This state is depicted in portraits of saints and yogis. This Being is "in the world but not of it," is comfortable in any situation, any circumstance, and lives in an imperturbable state of inner peace and happiness—dispassionately yet compassionately observing the play of life.

ACHIEVING THE MEDITATIVE STATE

For Tantra, or Kundalini, Yoga, the most important practices for developing the concentration and relaxed alertness necessary to achieve the meditative state are mantra japa and yantra meditation. The single most important practice to adhere to for as long as it takes is meditation—along with Self-inquiry. All of the great spiritual traditions teach the central role of meditation in seeing who we really are and ultimately transcending duality in the realization of eternal Truth—the knowledge that "I Am That." This is the Self as **Sat-Chit-Ananda**—Truth, Consciousness, Bliss—the highest state of existence.

ATTAINING SELF-REALIZATION

It is a rare being who attains the state of Self-realization. And when a person is fortunate enough to attain this state, she or he is spiritualized consciousness in a human body—no longer a consciousness separate from God-consciousness. This is Divine Energy in its fullest realization within the limitations of the human body. Any residual karma will dissolve in this lifetime. A Self-realized being no longer exists for herself or himself but only as Divine Will, as Divine Truth, as Divine Love, as **asamaprajnata samadhi** (eternal bliss). This is the ultimate goal of the spiritual path and the ultimate attainment for all human beings. When such a being drops the physical body, he or she knows when that time will be and can even choose the time. When the physical demise happens, the body is discarded like an old robe and the consciousness remains absorbed in the Divine Energy, with no residual separate consciousness to be reincarnated to live out its karma.

WORKBOOK EXERCISES

As with the previous chakras, read carefully through the Characteristics section and list any disorders—physical or psycho-spiritual—that particularly apply to you. In addition rate your current sense of well-being, relaxation, contentment, and acceptance. Remember that healing is not necessarily curing as it transcends the physical.

MANTRA PRACTICE—OM

Continue with the mantra practice on the Ajna chakra outlined in Chapter Nine. When you are very familiar with this practice, start to move toward mentally saying the **OM** (**AUM**) internally rather than sounding it out loud. This is a progressive practice.

1. After you have sounded the mantra out loud for some time, start to recite it softly, with the same focus of attention as in the more vocal recitation.
2. Then recite the mantra alternately softly and loudly.
3. Then recite it even more softly than before.
4. Then recite it silently and internally, maintaining the three areas of attention on the different vowels: the long "a" (as in a-a-a or ah-ah-ah), resonating in the abdomen around the navel area; the long "u" (as in o-o-o), moving the breath and attention to the middle of the chest—the Anahata chakra or spiritual Heart-center; and the long m-m-m, with a nasal resonance, in the area between the eyebrows—the third-eye area.
5. Maintain this practice of silently sounding the **OM** (**AUM**).

Someone who has reached the level of the Sahasrara chakra is usually able to hear the pranava **OM**—the internal **OM** sound heard by yogis and yoginis.

VISUALIZATION OF WHITE LIGHT

In addition to invoking the Divine "White Light," this practice further develops concentration and the state of relaxed alertness necessary to attain meditation. The practice is in two parts.

WHITE LIGHT VISUALIZATION: PART ONE

Adopt your meditation posture. Notice if there are any tense areas in the body. Breathe into them sequentially on the in breath and relax the tension on the out breath. When you are physically comfortable and relaxed, maintain stillness for the duration of the visualization/meditation.

Bring your focus of attention to the space between the eyebrows—the Ajna chakra area. Now visualize or imagine the spine as a hollow, transparent cylinder—as though made of clear glass. Begin to fill the cylinder with White Light—starting from the base, or Muladhara chakra area, and moving upward through the cylinder. Allow the passage of the White Light to rise up through the entire length of the cylinder. Hold this image for as long as you are able to without strain.

WHITE LIGHT VISUALIZATION: PART TWO

When the visualization practice is familiar, introduce attention to the breath.
With each inhalation, visualize taking in White Light.
With each exhalation, focus on the level of the Light.

Note in your Workbook Journal how you feel and the experiences/effects of the practice after each visualization session. Repeat the practice regularly until the visualization comes easily.

WORKBOOK EXERCISES

Look back at the questions asked at the beginning of this journey through the chakras (see page 21) and again read your responses. Now ask yourself these similar questions and note your responses in your Workbook Journal.

1. Reviewing the earlier questions, note what has changed for you—with each question.
2. How do you know what you now know?
3. In response to the question "Who am I?" asked of you throughout this book, what is your present perception of "I?" How has this changed?
4. What is the purpose of your life?
5. What is your definition of truth?
6. Define your spiritual beliefs.
7. List the ethical principles and values that now guide your everyday life.
8. What is the foundational support of your life?
9. Write down your principal sources of inspiration.
10. Write your personal definition of the words "knowledge" and "wisdom."
11. How do you serve others?
12. What is your perception of consciousness?
13. How would you describe your current state of being?
14. What is your definition of silence?
15. What is your perception of love?

Although the state of Self-realization is a wordless state existing beyond the mind in the realm of pure Consciousness, there are beautiful and moving accounts from those who have attained this state and, within the limits of language, have communicated the experience in scriptures, in mystical poetry, in stories, and in teachings from yogis and other spiritual teachers. These are fruitful and inspirational texts to seek out and heartwarming company on your journey.

Continue to note your experiences in response to your ongoing practices in your Workbook Journal and periodically review your notes as your journey continues.
Let the Light be your guide.

CHAPTER ELEVEN

CHAKRA THERAPIES IN THE WEST

How do the chakra system and yoga relate to other philosophies, particularly Reiki and the Kabbalah? Try hara breathing and a visualization on the Tree of Life.

As yoga, the chakra system, energy medicine, and related practices have become increasingly known in the West, methods not embedded in the yoga tradition have been introduced for working with the chakras. In 1875 the Theosophical Society was founded to advocate the universality of the perennial wisdom teachings—different spiritual paths that all reach toward the One Truth. In 1888 the Hermetic Order of the Golden Dawn, a Western magical group, began experimenting with visualizations using parallels between the Tree of Life in the Kabbalah (the mystical school of Judaism) and symbols from the chakra system.

With the advent of the New Age in the late 1960s, "chakra work" has increasingly been treated as a discrete modality. It also has been grafted onto existing systems such as the Japanese Reiki. Other methods, such as chakras and gemstones and chakras and labyrinths, are relatively new exercises, and while they can be nurturing in their own right, they bear no real connection to Tantra Yoga, which originated the system of working with the chakras and the spiritual Kundalini Shakti Energy.

THE CHAKRAS AND REIKI

Central to the modality of Reiki is working with Universal Energy. Reiki is essentially an energy healing technique using the systematic laying-on of hands. Specific symbols are also used in healing sessions. By a process of "attunements" by a Reiki master, a practitioner is enabled to act as a channel of Universal Energy for healing purposes.

Reiki was developed in Japan by Usui Sensei, a Zen Buddhist, in the 1920s. It began filtering into the West from the late 1930s. Since its move to the West, some practitioners have introduced chakra work into the Reiki system; however, no consistent principles have been established for the use of the chakra system of Kundalini Yoga within Reiki. In addition, the Reiki system works more on an understanding of hara—a powerfully concentrated energy point just below the navel in the human body. Traditionally, Japanese modalities have used the hara center rather than the chakra system as a method to stimulate and balance energy in the body.

HARA

The word *hara*—not to be confused with the Sanskrit and yogic meaning—means "belly" in Japanese; references to hara seem more widespread in Japan than in other cultures. There does seem to be one strong correspondence between the pranic system of Kundalini Yoga and other Eastern systems that work with hara. The description of the point of origin of the nadis in the human body, the "egg-shaped" kanda, appears to correspond to the Japanese meaning for hara. It is a "power spot" located three fingers below the navel—midway between the upper and lower bodies. It is considered to be the anchoring point at which the physical and subtle bodies are balanced and centered.

In preindustrial civilizations, which were centered in Mother Earth and more in harmony with natural forces, people were naturally centered in their bodies. There seemed to be a natural correlation between earth-connectedness and being centered in the belly. However, as societies have become increasingly masculinized and technologically advanced, people have become more centered in their rational minds and consequently in their upper bodies. This can be seen as weakening the organism and causing imbalances in the subtle and physical body–mind systems. Although yoga and Reiki are very different modalities with different pathways and practices, they both help to restore wholeness to the entire body–mind system by working with Universal Energy.

HARA BREATHING

As well as being an essential element of the Reiki system, the hara is well known in Buddhism, in the Tao, in martial arts, and for professional singing. All of these disciplines have practices for strengthening this energy center in the body. A simple and effective way of developing awareness and strengthening hara is through a simple technique called "hara breathing."

There are two stages to this breathing practice—first being able to sense, or locate, the hara in the body, and then the practice itself, whereby you increase your familiarity with hara and then can raise the energy stored there at will.

HARA BREATHING: PART ONE

Lie on your side if you can. If not, sit with a comfortable, stable posture. Maintain a straight spine as in meditation. Place your attention on an area about three fingers below your navel, and breathe naturally and deeply into this area. Continue breathing into this area for at least ten minutes and notice your responses. When you feel you have sensed/located this energy center, move to the second stage.

HARA BREATHING: PART TWO

Adopt a comfortable, stable sitting posture. It is important to keep your knees below your hips. Keep your spine straight, shoulders down and relaxed, and hands resting naturally on thighs. Breathe through your nose, and on the inhalation take the air down deep into your belly. Keep your chest still, and let your diaphragm extend out.

Now exhale, drawing in the belly, allowing your diaphragm to concertina naturally inward. This will circulate energy throughout your body. This is an excellent breathing exercise that can be done anywhere at any time. It will relax, center, ground, and energize you all at the same time.

THE CHAKRAS AND THE KABBALAH: THE TREE OF LIFE

Like the chakras, the Jewish mystical system of the Kabbalah is based on energy centers that are spiritual centers as well. As with the chakras, there is a progressive journey through the centers to attain higher spiritual consciousness. The Tree of Life is the composite symbol of the process of Creation and also the matrix containing the symbolic energy centers, called the *sephiroth*.

When these centers are visualized within the human body, they are seen as forming three vertical pillars (see diagram below). The base of the central pillar is associated with the feet, and the outer pillars align with the shoulders and arms. The table on page 180 shows how we can correlate the Kundalini Yoga chakras and the sephiroth on the central pillar of the Tree of Life. The two systems are quite different and separate, one belonging to an Eastern system and one to a Western, and it is not always appropriate to mix them.

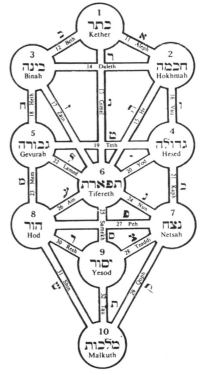

The central pillar, with its energy centers and the paths that connect them, is known as the Middle Pillar. The exercise known as the Middle Pillar exercise is a visualization to invoke spiritual Energy. Note, in the table on page 180, how the colors of the energy spheres differ for the two systems. The Middle Pillar exercise is outlined below as practiced by adherents of Kabbalism. However, to align this visualization loosely with yoga and the chakra system, reverse the path of this exercise and visualize the energy centers and their ascribed colors from Malkuth (Muladhara) upward, sphere by sphere, to the sacred source beyond Kether (Sahasrara). Use only the colors attributed to the sephiroth for the Middle Pillar exercise and only the colors attributed to the chakras for the chakra visualization.

THE CHAKRAS AND THE SPHERES ON
THE KABBALISTIC TREE OF LIFE

SEPHIRAH	COLOR	CHAKRA	TATTWA	COLOR
Malkuth	Dark green or black	Muladhara	Earth	Yellow/red
Yesod	Purple tinged with silver	Svadisthana	Water	Silver or orange, light blue or transparent
Tiphareth	Golden-yellow	Manipura	Fire	Red-gold or yellow-gold
Tiphareth	Golden-yellow	Anahata	Air	Green or smoke
Daath	Violet tinged with blue	Visuddha	Akasha/ether	Smoky purple or indigo
		Ajna		White or bluish-white
Kether	Pure white	Sahasrara		Colorless/refracted light: rainbow spectrum

THE MIDDLE PILLAR EXERCISE

The first activity in Western magical rituals is always to establish the sacred space—the magic circle—around you, so that you then activate the spiritual energies within your own sphere of consciousness. The exercise can be done standing.

1. Face the East and imagine a sphere of vibrant, pure white light radiating just above the crown of your head. After you have succeeded in focusing your awareness on this sphere of light, draw it down into the crown and vibrate the God-name AHIH (pronounced **eeh-hee-yay**). This is the visualization for the sphere of **Kether.**

2. Now draw this light down through the central axis of your body so that it reaches your throat. Visualize this energy center as a sphere of vibrant blue or violet light, and vibrate the God-name YHVH ELOHIM (pronounced **ye-ho-waah el-oh-hee**). This is the visualization for the sphere of **Daath.**

3. Bring the light down from your throat to the region of your solar plexus—in the region of your upper abdomen. Visualize this energy center as a sphere of vibrant golden-yellow light and vibrate the God-name YHVH ELOAH VA DAAT (pronounced **ye-ho-waah el-oh-ah va da-art**). This is the visualization for the sphere of **Tiphareth.**

4. Now draw the light down into the regions of your genitals. Visualize this energy center as a sphere of vibrant purple/silver light and vibrate the God-name SHADDAI EL CHAI (pronounced **shah-dai el kaii**). This is the visualization for the sphere of **Yesod.**

5. Here is the final step, but if you want to align the exercise with your chakra work, begin here and work backward. Bring the light down to the soles of your feet and imagine it is spreading out beneath your feet to form a perfect circle. Traditionally this sphere is associated with a grouping of earth colors—russet, olive, citrine, and black. If you find it difficult visualizing this cluster of colors, visualize the sphere as very dark green or black and vibrate the God-name ADNI HA ARETZ (pronounced **aah-doh-naii haa ah-retz**). This is the visualization for the sphere of **Malkuth.**

It is said in the Kabbalah that *Ain Soph Aur*—the Infinite Light and "Innermost Being of God"—is the Bridegroom of Shekinah, the Bride, or Queen. She is the equivalent, in the Kabbalah, of the Universal Mother—the feminine face of God. Her home is in the sphere of Malkuth, symbolized by the element earth, a center of feminine energy. By raising the sacred light from Malkuth and bringing it back to Kether and beyond, we are ritually performing the Kabbalistic equivalent of the sacred union of Kundalini Shakti and Shiva.

Try the exercises suggested in this chapter, and if they resonate for you, see the Further Reading list for starting points on the discipline of Reiki or the Kabbalah philosophy.

AFTERWORD

I am beyond concept, beyond form.
I am all pervading in all the senses.
I see equality in all things. I am neither liberated nor in bondage.
I am eternal bliss. I am Shiva.
From a traditional Hindu mantra called "Chidananda" (Eternal Bliss)

The ancient sages of India understood that the ultimate goal of human life is Self-realization or God-realization. This meant living a life that is beyond ego or sense-gratification and one that is energetically balanced, moderate, self-disciplined, nonmaterialistic, and organized around the achievement of a goal. This is where true yoga begins. For the ancient rishis, yoga was living wisdom, not a periodic pastime.

Pursuing any spiritual path requires commitment to regular practice. If you are using the chakras as a path to Self-realization, essential components of this practice are both meditation and an ethical code of living. Such a code is Patanjali's eight limbs of yoga—the most important "limb" being *yama* (moral restraint), which includes ahimsa (nonharming), truthfulness, sexual restraint, moderation, non-acquisitiveness, and kindness. The teachings of shamanism—the world's oldest religion—the dharma teachings of Buddhism, the Sufi teachings of Islam, and the true teachings and commandments of Christ are other examples. The principles of these disciplines were laid down in ancient times, but they can allow the seeker who lives in today's multicultural or pluralistic cultures to remain true to the essence of their enlightened teachings.

It is not easy to discard our past negative patterning and live consistently in an ethical, honorable, and congruent way at the same time as maintaining a spontaneous enjoyment of life, but it is essential if we aspire to spiritual development and higher levels of awareness.

For spiritual work we need stamina, commitment, honesty, resilience, and the ability to endure—toughness as well as tenderness. These are qualities we develop as we do the work. We all experience difficulties, obstacles, challenges, and fear. Facing a reality in a climate of self-respect and self-acceptance, and letting it take its own healing course, is not the same as forcing a process or an outcome. It is sometimes helpful to remind ourselves how we all were as infants when learning a new skill. We tried, we fell down, we got up and tried again, and all the time we were getting stronger, we were learning, even if we did not realize it until later.

Using this book will help you to incorporate your beliefs and practices in everyday life in all you encounter—both from without and from within. As the wisdom inherent in Native American cultures espouses, "you have to walk the talk." This is not to say that life is serious business and there is not a place for lightness of being. On the contrary, a robust sense of humor and a warmly empathic and compassionate attitude toward all—including ourselves—is good medicine.

To quote Sri Bhagavan Ramana Maharshi:
Better than viewing God as Other, the noblest attitude is to view God as "The 'I' within,
The very 'I'... Absorption in the heart of being, whence we sprang, is the path of action,
of devotion, of union, and of knowledge.

And, to quote another great sage, Mevlana Jelaluddin Rumi:
The breeze at dawn has secrets to tell you. Don't go back to sleep. You must ask for what
you really want. Don't go back to sleep... The door is round and open. Don't go back to
sleep.

FURTHER READING

Avalon, Arthur (Sir John Woodruffe), *The Serpent Power*, Dover Publications, New York, 7th edition, 1974.

Brennan, Barbara Ann, *Hands of Light*, Bantam Books, New York, 1988.

Gerber, Richard, *Vibrational Medicine*, Bear & Company, Sante Fe, New Mexico, 1988.

Johari, Harish, *Chakras, Energy Centers of Transformation*, Destiny Books, Rochester, Vermont, 1987.

Judith, Anodea, *Wheels of Life*, Llewellyn Publications, Minnesota, 1996.

———. *Eastern Body, Western Mind*, Celestial Arts, Berkeley, California, 1996.

Khalsa, Guru Dharam Singh, and O'Keefe, Darryl, *Kundalini, The Essence of Yoga*, Gaia Books, London, 2002.

Khalsa, Shakti Parwha Kaur, *Kundalini Yoga*, Dorling Kindersley, New York, 2001.

Krishna, Gopi, *Kundalini, The Evolutionary Energy in Man*, Shambhala Publications, Berkeley, California, 1971.

———. *The Secret of Yoga*, Turnstone Books, London, 1972.

Leadbeater, Charles W., *The Chakras*, The Theosophical Publishing House, Adyar, Madras, 1927, 1996.

Matt, Daniel C., *The Essential Kabbalah*, Castle Books, Edison, New Jersey, 1997.

Motoyama, Hiroshi, *Theories of the Chakras*, Quest Books, Illinois, 1981.

Mumford, Dr. Jonn, *Chakra & Kundalini Workbook*, Llewellyn Publications, Minnesota, 1994.

Radha, Swami Sivananda, *Kundalini Yoga for the West*, Shambhala Publications, Boulder, Colorado, 1981.

Stein, Diane, *The Essential Reiki*, Crossing Press, Freedom, California, 1995.

White, John, *Kundalini, Evolution and Enlightenment*, Paragon House, Minnesota, 1990.

GLOSSARY

Ahamkara—the ego, I-consciousness

Ahimsa—nonviolence, nonharming

Ajna—command, command wheel (sixth chakra)

Akasha—space, void, ether

Amrit/amrita—nectar of immortality

Anahata—unstruck (Heart chakra, fourth chakra)

Anahata nada—the primal cosmic sound

Anahata-sabda—the unstruck sound

Ananda—bliss

Artha—wealth

Asamaprajnata samadhi—eternal bliss, supreme Consciousness

Asana—posture

Bana Lingam—Shiva lingam (in Anahata chakra)

Bhakti—devotion

Bija mantra—seed sound (see page 38)

Bindu—the ultimate Truth from which all manifest form arises, the dot above the crescent on the sacred syllable OM

Brahma—God of Creation, one of three principal Gods of Indian spirituality

Brahma Granthi—the knot of Brahma (in Manipura chakra), see also **granthi**

Brahman—the One Ultimate Truth, formless reality, the Godhead

Chakra (cakra)—wheel, disk, vortice of vital pranic energy

Deva—male deity

Devi—female deity

Dharma—principles of right living

Ganesha—elephant-headed god, remover of obstacles

Granthi—knot, aspect of consciousness

Gunas—qualities

Hamsah—individual soul

Hrit—heart

Itara Lingam—Shiva lingam (in the Ajna chakra)

Jalandhara bandha—chin lock

Jiva—individual self

Kama—celebration of beauty

Kanda (or *kandasthana*)—bulb, origination point of nadis

Karma—universal law of cause and effect

Kosha—envelope, sheath

Kundalini/Kundalini Shakti—she who is coiled, Shakti (Power) in the image of a serpent lying dormant in Muladhara (the first chakra)

Lila—divine sport or play

Lingam—male sex organ, symbol of Shiva

Manas—mind

Manipura—gem, dwelling place, navel (the third chakra)

Mantra—repeated word or phrase, use of sound to develop concentration

Mantra japa—mantra repetition

Moksha—ultimate liberation

Mudra—symbolic gesture to assist meditation

Muladhara—root, support (the first/root chakra)

Nada—pure cosmic sound

Nada-bindu—primordial sound vibration from which the universe was formed

Nadis—a system of energy channels or conduits for prana

OM *(AUM)*—the source of all sound, the sacred syllable seed sound that continues infinitely

Padma—lotus

Parama Hamsah—Supreme Self

Prana—vital life-force energy

Pranava—OM (AUM)

Pranayama—conscious breath control

Rajas—passion, activity

Rishi—seer, saint, holy person

Rudra Granthi—the knot of Rudra (in Ajna chakra)

Sabda Brahman—the Absolute in the form of sound

Sa'Ham—I Am She/I Am That

Sahasrara—thousand-spoke wheel (seventh chakra)

Samadhi—a state of blissful Self-realization

Sat-Chit-Ananda—Truth–Consciousness –Bliss

Sattva—purity, light

Shakti—Power, Energy, dynamic creative aspect of Shiva

Shiva (Siva)—the destroyer aspect of God, pure Consciousness, one of the three principal Gods of Indian spirituality

Siddhis—psychic powers, super powers

So'Ham—I Am He/I Am That

Soma—nectar

Soma chakra—chakra/lotus within the Sahasrara chakra

Svadisthana—abode of the self, our own abode (the second chakra)

Svayambu Lingam—Shiva lingam (in Muladahara chakra)

Swami—a holy person

Tamas—darkness, inertia

Tantra—expand consciousness

Tattwa/tattva—element

Trimurti—the Hindu Trinity (of Brahma, Vishnu, and Shiva)

Tripura—three worlds (see page 61)

Upanishads—texts containing the essence of the Vedas

Vedas—ancient Hindu scriptures, sacred teachings

Vishnu—God of Preservation, second God in the Hindu Trinity

Vishnu Granthi—the knot of Vishnu (in Anahata chakra)

Visuddha—pure wheel (the fifth chakra)

Yama—moral restraint

Yantra—shape, pattern, symbolic diagram for meditation

Yoga—a system of practices to relax the body and mind, purify the system, and remove energy blockages. Literal translation: to yoke, unite, join

Yogi/yogini—yoga adept

Yoni—symbol of female sex organ

INDEX

QUICK REFERENCE GUIDE

Sahasrara—the seventh chakra, pages 166–175

Ajna—the sixth chakra, pages 150–165

Visuddha—the fifth chakra, pages 128–149

Anahata—the fourth chakra, pages 108–127

Manipura—the third chakra, pages 90–107

Svadisthana—the second chakra, pages 70–89

Muladhara—the first chakra, pages 50–69